Practical Problems

Ten Stories for the Stage

Practical Problems

Ten Stories for the Stage

J. Ajlouny

Fresh Ink Group
Guntersville

Practical Problems:
Ten Stories for the Stage

Fresh Ink Group
An Imprint of:
The Fresh Ink Group, LLC
1021 Blount Avenue #931
Guntersville, AL 35976
Email: info@FreshInkGroup.com
FreshInkGroup.com

Edition 1.0   2022

Cover design by Stephen Geez / FIG
Book design by Amit Dey / FIG
Associate publisher Lauren A. Smith / FIG

Cataloging-in-Publication Recommendations:
PER011030 PERFORMING ARTS / Theater / Playwriting
PER020000 PERFORMING ARTS / Monologues & Scenes
PER019000 PERFORMING ARTS / Storytelling

Library of Congress Control Number: 20226971521

ISBN-13: 978-1-947893-73-3 Papercover
ISBN-13: 978-1-947893-65-8 Hardcover
ISBN-13: 978-1-947893-61-0 Ebooks

Table of Contents

Introduction

These ten plays were written over a period of about fifteen years. Each was inspired by some event that influenced me in some way and motivated me to tell it as a story. I wrote a handful of others, mostly for theatre companies of which I was a member, but I couldn't find copies. Perhaps it's just as well, for theatre is an ephemeral art form. Once a show's run is finished, so too is the show itself. Of course, the exception to this is the touring production, which performs the same show over and over again as long as audiences will pay to enjoy it. But even for popular plays that are regularly presented, like those of Shakespeare, O'Neill or Albee, each production is unique and ends its existence when the final curtain falls. That's the bittersweet nature of theatre. Every show is a beginning and an end. That's what makes live performance so different than recorded entertainment. A movie on DVD never changes; a play, a dance, a concert always does and that's what makes each iteration unique.

These stories for the stage are diverse tales but when I attempted to analyze them as I re-edited each for this collection, I found that in each one, the characters were experiencing various kinds of personal challenges, as we all do every day of our blessed lives. Mind you, I was not searching for a unifying theme, just a title for the collection. They tell you in playwriting school, create appealing characters, good or bad, give them some conflict, place them on a journey and then allow them to resolve it in a credible manner. That's fine and dandy for learning the craft, but it's awfully formulaic and I detest formulaic writing. I also detest routine living. So, I sought to resist the expectation that my stories be predictable or routine tales. I wanted them to be realistic, witty, probative and moving. But mostly, I want them to be entertaining. I believe these ten plays satisfy that ambition.

To obviate the need to summarize them here, I gave each a one-line synopsis beneath its title and that should suffice to give you the flavor of the thing. I made sure each was easy to cast and stage and inexpensive to produce. That's important in theatre. It's also important to keep them brief and to the point. There is nothing worse than sitting through a play that suffers on senselessly, unaware of its burdensome nature. The actors may be immune to it, but the audience never is. And I trust the audience.

How I developed an abiding interest in theatre I cannot say. But I know it started early. I recall playing Peter Cottontail in elementary school. And I recall playing a hood in Bea Kaufman's once-popularly presented school drama, *Up the Downstairs Case* when I was in middle school. And I remember working as a sound and lighting technician for our high school productions of *West Side Story* and *Guys and Dolls*. A singer and dancer I am not! By the time I graduated, I had written several plays, but I don't remember any of them except one, which I called Travels with Pete and Judy. It was about a young couple who bored their friends with tales of their travels around the world and how they acted out scenes in distant lands that they had captured in their photographs. I remember clanging it out on my old pipe-organ of a typewriter and using those chalk sheets to correct my mistakes. The next one I recall, I wrote while I was in college. It was called *Please, Mr. President*. It was the first play I wrote on a word processor, which was some years before the introduction of the PC. It was the story of a

U.S. president who locked himself in the Oval Office and communicated to his White House staff, indeed, to the world via closed-circuit TV. This play was produced once at a local community theatre for a two-weekend run. It didn't receive any reviews, that I can remember. That was before the days of VHS too so I never had a filmed copy of it either. Just as well. It probably deserves to be totally forgotten.

The only other play I can remember writing that I cannot find a copy of (there were others I'm sure but I can't remember them at all) was called *The Mystery of Cupcake O'Malley* about a popular torch singer in the 1950's who disappeared without a trace. The play is in the form of a documentary-style investigation, together with a dozen long-forgotten songs I unearthed which I thought were lovely and deserved to be heard again. It was performed in a staged reading format with the songs sung in a concert setting. I've never seen anything like that attempted again. Perhaps that's a fitting elegy for it. Oh, for the record, the singer became a nun and made a vow of obedience and silence. So her disappearance was bittersweet and not a tragedy.

These ten stories for the stage all postdate those. Just as well because maybe learned a thing or two about the craft of playwriting. And perhaps that learning is evident here. I suppose I could have written each as a short story but that struck me as giving them short shrift. I've always felt a kind of maudlin compassion for books that just rest on shelves and are never actually held and read. I wanted these characters to come alive, even if they never did. They could. They might, and that is good enough for me.

J. Ajlouny
May 2022

Goin' Legit

Goin' Legit

**Mobsters attempt to apply for a bank
loan to finance their criminal enterprise**

TIME:	Spring 1925
PLACE:	Detroit
SETTING:	Office of the vice president of the loans and mortgage department of First Bank and Trust of Detroit

CHARACTERS:

Franklin Ralston: Banker, mid-60's

Charlie "The Bone" Bonanatto;   James Cagney-like mob boss

Kid Corelli: Typical wise guy; on the dumb side

Big Jimbo: Big and strong; menacing enforcer-type

AT OPENING: Banker Franklin Ralston is at his desk, leaning back in his chair and speaking on the phone.

*   *   *

Ralston

Speaking on the phone in a jovial mood.

Hey that's a good one Harry. I always get a kick out of those farmer-who-had-a-daughter jokes. Maybe one day I'll be lucky enough to run out of gas near a farm like that, especially since I intend to do a lot of cross-country road trips in my retirement. When's my last day you ask? A week from this Friday. It seems to make sense to make it at the end of the month since it's also the end of the third quarter. You know us bankers think in terms of quarterly reports and quarterly results. It's gonna be a nice feather in my cap to go out with record profits that we're gonna announce Wednesday. What's that Harry, inside information? You didn't hear that from me, did ya ole boy. Well, I gotta get back to work; I have an appointment scheduled in just a few minutes. Don't forget to bring your wife to the retirement party. We'll be looking forward to seeing you both. Yeah that's right. Okay, see you on Friday at the club. And remember no gifts please, unless of course you can mix it with tonic and pour it over ice. Good talkin' to you Harry, see ya soon.

He hangs up and flips through papers on his desk, reviewing documents and taking notes. His phone rings and he answers it.

Okay that's fine Miss Jones, show them in, I'm ready.

The door to his office opens and in walk three men, each of whom is dressed classic 1920's mobster attire. The first to enter is obviously the boss and the others are his henchmen. Franklin stands up and greets them one by one.

Gentlemen, welcome. Right on time too. I always admire businessmen who are punctual. It says a lot about character I always say.

Kid Corelli

Maybe that's why's people always call me a character, hey Boss?

Charlie the Bone

Quiet you birdbrain. We want to make a good impression here on ah Mister umm…Mister ah….

Ralston

Ralston, Franklin Ralston. Franklin Ralston III actually.

Charlie the Bone

You don't say. You mean there are two other of ya"s?

Kid Corelli

It don't pay to be a stool pigeon does it Boss?

Charlie the Bone

It pays plenty….If you like your belly full of lead.

Kid Corelli

Yeah Boss, that's for sure. Wise guys always wind up costing us a fortune in lead.

Charlie the Bone

That's okay kid; they earned it, didn't they?

Kid Corelli

They sure did Boss. That's what happens when you don't have a positive altitude, huh Boss?

Charlie the Bone

That's right kid. But we're being rude to Mister ah….

Ralston

Ralston, Franklin Ralston at your service gentlemen, and you must be Mr. Charles Bonanatto *Pronouncing it slowly "Bo-na-nat-to"*

Did I say that right?

Charlie the Bone

That's good enough but everyone calls me "The Bone" for short. It's kind of an alias...

Means nickname

Kid Corelli

Charlie The Bone. Maybe you heard of him Mr. Ralston?

Ralston

I think perhaps I have. Are you in the lumber business maybe? Or is it trucking?

Charlie the Bone

Lumber, trucking, taxis, distribution, retail, wholesale, you name it, I'm in it. See?

Ralston

That's fine; my late father always said the key to success in business is diversification. You certainly sound like you are.

Charlie the Bone

Diversification huh, I like the sound of that. Am I really?

Ralston

Turning to Kid Corelli

And you are, sir?

Kid Corelli

I'm not a sir, sir. I'm just a kid. Kid Corelli at your service.

They shake hands for longer than necessary.

Ralston

Welcome Mr. Corelli.

Kid Corelli

You can call me Kid. Everybody else does.

Ralston

And this gentleman is……

Motioning to Big Jimbo, who is standing cross-armed at the door, like a sentry. Ralston extends his hand to shake Big Jimbo's hand, but Big Jimbo doesn't respond.

Nice to meet you.

Charlie the Bone

Don't mind him, that's Big Jimbo. He doesn't like to talk.

Kid Corelli

At least not with his mouth. He lets his dukes does his talkin' for him. If ya know what I mean?

I see. The strong silent type, I guess you could say.

Charlie the Bone

Except when he nods off. He snores louder than a black bear. Sheesh!

Kid Corelli

Yeah, you could say it is "unbear-able!" Right boss?

Charlie the Bone

You could say that birdbrain. At least we know he'll never sing, that's for sure.

Kid Corelli

For sure boss, ain't nobody gonna make Jimbo sing. No how, no way, never. Right Jimbo?

Big Jimbo

Growls like a bear.

Kid Corelli

Never!

Ralston

Well gentlemen, to what do I owe the honor of your presence here today?

Charlie the Bone

Oh you don't owe us anything…at least not yet.

Ralston

I mean what can our bank do you? I presume you are interested in a business loan of some kind. Perhaps a line of credit? How can we be of service?

Charlie the Bone

Now you're talkin' Mr. Ralston.

Ralston

Please call me Franklin.

Charlie the Bone

Can I make it Frankie, for short?

Ralston

Of course you can.

Charlie the Bone

Good. I once knew a guy from Toledo named Frankie. He was a real fine mug. You sort of look like him, in a funny kind of way.

Kid Corelli

'Cept Frankie had a scar across his face he got from a run-in with a straight razor. Couldn't happened to a nicer guy. But the doctor patched it up pretty good though, at the same time he's got his fingertips wiped clean.

Charlie the Bone

The old double-o, works every time!

Ralston

I see. Well why don't you take a seat and make yourselves comfortable. Tell me how much did you have in mind? To borrow I mean.

Charlie the Bone

Well, the way I see it Frankie, we needs enough dough to buy three swell new boats for our importin' enterprise.

Ralston

Boats you say. You mean ships?

Charlie the Bone

I wouldn't call 'em that ca-sactly. More like speed boats. More like speed boats. Fast boats that beat Coast Guard boats.

Kid Corelli

And quiet-like too. Nothin' worser than a loud boat bringing all kinds of unwanted contention to it.

Ralston

Have you researched which model you want?

Charlie the Bone

Oh sure. Our Chicago partners gave us the specifications - like the word huh? - And we put 'em for a bid. We got three boat builders interested in the contract. We like the Germans but we're leaning towards the Polacks on account of our respect for Killer Kowalski and his gang.

Ralston

Killer Kowalski? Is he a former boxer? I seem to recall…

Kid Corelli

Nah, I think you're getting him mixed up with Killer Kowalchick, you know, the guy who you's could persuade to take a dive if you was in a pinch.

Charlie the Bone

That's right. The last dive he took was in the Detroit River…

Kid Corelli

…with cement boots, right boss?

Charlie the Bone

Quiet you pee-brain. You don't want Frankie here to think we go in for fixed bouts, do ya?

Kid Corelli

Is dare any other kind boss?

Charlie the Bone

Please just call me "The Bone." All my friends do.

Kid Corelli

And his enemies does too!

Ralston

Okay, Mr. Bone. About these boats. You're going to be using them to transport cargo I presume.

Charlie the Bone

Bingo Frankie! Now you're talkin'; cargo, that's the ticket. I like that. We're gonna be importin' cargo…from across the river.

Ralston

Oh, from Canada?

Charlie the Bone

Windsor, yeah, you got it!

Kid Corelli

Yeah, they speak fluid English there too.

Ralston

Fluid English, you don't say. May I ask what kind of goods?

Kid Corelli

Good goods, if ya knows what I mean.

He gestures drinking.

Ralston

Oh…Oh. You mean those kinds of goods.

Charlie the Bone

That's where the demand is Frankie; and Windsor has got the supply.

Ralston

So you'll become the middlemen, so to speak.

Charlie the Bone

Middleman, yeah, I like that. I'm gonna become the middleman.

Kid Corelli

Is that anything like the man in the middle Boss?

Charlie the Bone

I think so kid. It's good to be wise to the parlance of high finance. Eh Frankie?

Ralston

Ah, yes Mr. Bone. Of course. And Ah…tell me…how much do you expect these boats will cost?

Charlie the Bone

I figure about 25 G's by the time they are properly outfitted, if ya know what I mean.

Ralston

25 G's…I mean thousand. I see. Well, that shouldn't be too difficult to secure. You understand the boats will need to be used as collateral to secure the debt of course.

Charlie the Bone

Of course. We understand. Collateral. I like the word.

Ralston

Do you have an enterprise name picked out? So I can begin filling out the loan application.

Charlie the Bone

Oh, we don't need nothin' in writin' Frankie. A handshake is good enough for us. See?

Ralston

You understand Mr. Bone that the bank needs proper documentation for all its loans, or our Loan Committee won't consider any application for a loan without all the proper documentation, including insurance contracts and purchase orders and the like.

Charlie the Bone

The only insurance we need is Big Jimbo and his Gang of Gorillas from Downriver.

Kid Corelli

Lots of muscle downriver!

Ralston

I understand gentlemen, but a bank is required to do things according to regulations. Surely you understand that.

Charlie the Bone

Of course we understand Frankie ole boy. Which is exactly why we came to you. You're a big player here. Louie the Lion told us you play fair, see? He said you could take care of us for a little piece of the action, say 2 percent for 24 months. Huh?

Kid Corelli

And 'dat ain't chicken feed Frankie. Cashola!

Money-gestures his fingers.

On da' barrelhead.

Ralston

Now gentlemen. Of course, I appreciate your confidence in me but there's only so much I can do. Surely yous... I mean... you understand. Rules is rules...are rules.

Charlie the Bone

You're not going soft on us, is ya Frankie? Louie the Lion said you like to play ball, not hard ball.

Ralston

Baseball, I think he meant.

Charlie the Bone

Now lookie here Frankie. We're trying to go legit here. This is a bank ain't it? Yous guys gots loads of money in those safes, don't ya?

Ralston

Mr. Bones, that money belongs to our depositors. We hold it for them as a fiduciary trustee. We can't just dole it out on a handshake and a promise to pay it back. Why the whole system would collapse and where would we be then?

Kid Corelli

I don't know wheres?

Ralston

In the poorhouse, that's where.

Kid Corelli

Like the one over on Porter street. My uncle used to stay there while he was on parole. But now he's back in the joint when the Hudson Motors payroll caper went south. That's what happens when your mugs try to chisel ya out of your share. They got what they had comin' to em', good ole Uncle Pete, you'd never wanna double cross a better mug.

Charlie the Bone

That's enough about your uncle, he should have known better then to hang with those Pittsburg rats. Nothin' good ever came out of Pittsburg but cold hard steel.

Ralston

Yes, well gentlemen. I'm sorry to say it doesn't look like we're going to be able to assist you. I wish I could recommend a ......

Charlie the Bone

What'd ya mean you ain't gonna be able to assist us. That ain't what Louie the Lion told us. And he oughta know.

Kid Corelli

Yeah, they don't call him The Lion for nuthin! He's long in the tooth if ya knows what I means.

Charlie the Bone

Very long! Hey kid, maybe he gave us a bum steer so he could muscle in on our action.

Kid Corelli

Yeah, take a-vantage of a delay.

Charlie the Bone

Maybe you're right kid. He ain't a lion, he's a snake! We'll give em what he's got coming to him. Make a note of that Big Jimbo.

Big Jimbo

Nods and growls.

Then takes a notepad out of his breast pocket, licks the tip of his pencil and jots a note to himself, he growls again.

Kid Corelli

I tell ya Boss, them Sicilians is really somethin'.

Charlie the Bone

Yeah. But nothin' that a foot of lead pipe couldn't solve.

Big Jimbo

Growls in assent.

Ralston

Gentlemen, please. We can't have the bank involved in any unsavory dealings if you know what I mean.

Charlie the Bone

Yeah, we got ya Frankie, stir-ickly on the Q.T. That's how we like to do business too.

Kid Corelli

Yeah, hush-hush. The old double H. Works every time.

Ralston

I don't think you gentlemen understand. The bank can't assist in any transaction that is not strictly above board, so to speak, surely you understand?

Charlie the Bone

I see Frankie, I understand. Two percent isn't heavy enough for ya. Hey kid, I like this guy. He's playin' tough that's all. I get it. Okay Frankie. My ears are open. Name your price. I ain't no tightwad.

Kid Corelli

Ya' sure ain't boss. You're a lot of things but tight wad sure ain't one of 'em.

Charlie the Bone

Quiet down bean breath, can't ya see we're in the middle of nee-go-she-a-tions here.

Kid Corelli

Sure Boss, I ain't sayin' a word. I'm zipping my trap startin' right now.

Gestures zipping his mouth.

Charlie the Bone

Standing up and leaning over the desk.

As I was saying Frankie old boy. What's your idea of fairness here? Remember, our Chicago partners don't mess around. When they say jump we ask how high, got it Frank? Ya' see?

Ralston

Ah, ah, I think so. Let me get this straight. You need 25 G's. You need it fast and with no paperwork, is that correct?

Charlie the Bone

Now you're talkin'. See that ain't so hard is it Frank? In cash of course!

Ralston

Of course I'll have to discuss it with our president and our chairman you understand. A transaction like this needs proper authorization.

He brings his fingers to his lips, hush hush-like.

Charlie the Bone

A-thor-i-za-tion, I like that word. Makes me feel important. Like a good customa'. "A-thor-i-za-tion."

Kid Corelli

It's a great word boss! Great word!

Ralston

And that could take ten days or so.

Charlie the Bone

Ten days? We ain't got that much time Frankie. I thought you understood.

He stands up.

See?

Ralston

Of course. Well let's see. Let me look at my calendar. Today is Thursday. Tomorrow is out of the question and Monday we're closed for auditing. Tuesday the loan committee meets. Wednesday the new interest rates will be published, Thursday I can meet with bosses. How about next Friday? I could let you know by next Friday.

Charlie the Bone

Well if that's the soonest we can get the dough…..

Ralston

Yes, absolutely earliest date possible.

Charlie the Bone

Well, I guess that's okay. But what do ya mean "interest" Frankie? What's interest between friends? We grease palms, that's our idea of interest.

Ralston

I understand entirely. I'll take it up with my boss. I'm sure we can arrive at a solution that'll be agreeable to all.

Charlie the Bone

Don't let us have to turn the nee-go-the-a-tions over to Big Jimbo and ….

Ralston

…. the Downriver Gorillas…no, of course not. There's no need for that kind of persuasion.

Big Jimbo

Growls.

Ralston

I think we can see eye to eye on this deal. And I appreciate your patience. I can assure you it'll be worth the wait.

Charlie the Bone

Now you're talkin' Frankie. That's what I like to hear. After all banking is just another racket, right Kid?

Kid Corelli

Sure boss, technee-cality speaking.

Ralston

Right, right. Well what do you say we make an appointment to meet next Friday at say 10 am? Is that acceptable to you gentlemen?

Charlie the Bone

Yeah, sounds good. We'll be here. Make a note of it Jimbo.

Big Jimbo

Writes a note in his pad, and growls.

Ralston

Well I want to thank you gentlemen for coming by today. Have a great weekend and spend next week finalizing your plans with the boat builder and that kind of stuff. Never waste an hour because you'll never get back, my father always used to say.

Charlie the Bone

I like that Frankie. Never waste an hour. I'll remember that one. Gosh, I'll bet your pops was a made-man.

Kid Corelli

No kiddin' ?

Ralston

Thank you gentlemen. Until next Friday. I look forward to seeing you then. Good bye.

He ushers them out of the office.

Charlie the Bone

Too-ta-loo Frankie Ol' boy. See ya next Friday. And always remember, anytime you need someone framed, bumped-off, or rubbed-out, we is at your service.

Kid Corelli

Yeah, anytime! Until next Friday, 10 am. The donuts is on us. A little jester on our part to say thanks, Pal.

Ralston

That'll be great gentlemen. Have a good day.

They exit.

Ralston paces back and forth nervously and makes nervous wheezing sounds.

I got it!

He picks up his phone.

Miss Jones. I've decided to make my last day on the job next Thursday, can you see to that? You can? Fantastic, Thursday it is! My final day of work. I'm gonna enjoy sleeping-in on Friday morning. No, on second thought I better catch a train Thursday evening, just to be safe. I hear them Downriver Gorillas is murda', Sheer murda'!

THE END

The Bright Side

The Bright Side

A minor incident escalates into a federal case

(Adapted from an idea from the Ziegfeld Follies Revue of 1925.)

TIME: 1950, Autumn

PLACE: Detroit

SETTING: A public park

CHARACTERS:

    Man #1: Short and middle-aged

    Man #2: Tall and middle-aged

    Police Officer: in uniform

AT OPENING: Two gentlemen are strolling and enjoying each other's company. They are casually dressed but wearing attire and hats fitting the era. They sit on a bench for a rest.

*   *   *

Man #1

So what did you think of the frolic last night? Did you enjoy yourself? I sure did.

Man #2

It was okay. Two of the three one-acts were tolerable and the dinner wasn't cold so by player's standards I'd say it was a success. Those new shoes I was telling you about were too tight and when I got home and removed them I had to soak my feet in Epsom salts.

Man #1

Well you can't blame that on the frolic.

Man #2

No but if I didn't have to walk up and down all those steps I wouldn't have had the chafing above my heels. Can't you tell how I've been favoring my feet all afternoon?

Man #1

No I hadn't noticed. I prefer to take in the beauty of the day not your fallen arches.

Man #2

Oh don't get me started on those. Or my corns. They're murder!

Man #1

Thank god you don't have hammer-toe.

Man #2

But I do and it's no picnic in the park I can tell you! My podiatrist wants to operate. Hammer-toe Joe I call him!

Man #1

Well?

Man #2

Are you kidding? He wants $400 and I'd have to stay off my feet for a week. Who on earth can afford that? Not me!

Man #1

Well it would sure give you a chance to let your swelling go down.

Man #2

Yea, maybe you're right, and the chafing too.

Man #1

And then while you're at it you could stretch those new shoes so they don't bother you again.

Man #2

Yeah, I could. Think of what I'd save in Epsom salts.

Man #1

And hot water!

Man #2

Yeah... Hey maybe I could write a will for him for the $400.

Man #1

Or maybe he needs a divorce.

Man #2

Yeah or maybe he needs to negotiate his lease.

Man #1

Or sue a patient for $400 for welching on a hammer toe operation.

Man #2

Yeah, wouldn't that be ironic. That's my idea of justice.

Man #1

Pulls a cigar out of his pocket and offers it to his friend but he declines it.

No?

Man #2

Are you kidding, after inhaling all that cigarette and cigar smoke last night I wouldn't dare. The coughing made my lumbago act up.

Man #1

You don't say?

Man #2 nods and grunts in pain. Man #1 bites the tip of the cigar off and spits it out on the ground. A police officer who was ambling by sees him do it, stops; stares at him with an air of disapproval and walks up to Man #1.

Man #1

Yes, officer? Lovely afternoon we're having isn't it?

Police Officer

It certainly is. But it's a whole lot less lovely when we have people spitting on the ground without a thought about the spreading of germs and filth. Wouldn't you agree?

Man #1

Well I suppose, you're right officer. I didn't think....

Police Officer

Of course you didn't think! There's a $2 fine for that you know.

Man #1

No I didn't know. Ah, listen; can we just keep this between the two of us? There's no reason to take this little incident to court, is there?

Police Officer

I'm afraid I haven't any choice. I'll have to write you a ticket and issue you a summons.

Man #1

Oh please ah, officer. Let me just give you the $2 and you can take care of it yourself without any further paperwork...if you know what I mean?

Police Officer

Are you attempting to bribe a police officer sir?

Man #1

Of course not. I just thought we could keep things simple, that's all. Please officer.

He searches his pocket for cash but comes up empty.

Hey, let me borrow two bucks will ya?

Man #2

Nothing doing. This officer is out of line. I didn't see you spit. Do you have any witnesses my good man? I don't think so!

Police Officer

Listen here buster.

Man #2

Don't "Buster" me, I pay your salary.

Police Officer

Do you now?

Man #2

I certainly do. And my friend here is on personal terms with the police commissioner.

Police Officer

You don't say.

Man #2

Isn't that true old friend? In fact, he was at the Players just last night, sitting across the aisle from us, and I can tell you he had a great time too.

Man #1

Let's keep the commissioner out of this. Just give the man $2 would ya.

Man #2

Not a chance. What kind of lawyer do you think I am?

Man #1

It's only $2. It's not worth arguing over. Just pay him the $2. Please. We have a golf game later this afternoon. We don't want to be late for our tee time do we?

Man #2

What's a tee time when we are dealing with the principle of the thing, like here? I'm telling the officer, run along and we'll forget this intrusion.

Police Officer

Intrusion?

Man #2

You'll leave us no choice but to contact the commissioner and report this harassment.

Police Officer

Harassment?

Man #1

Now listen fellas. Let's not let this get out of hand. Let's just be practical. Pay him the $2 and let's get out of here. I'll buy you lunch at the club.

Man #2

This matter is already out of hand. First he falsely accuses you of spitting in public and then he falsely accuses you of attempting to bribe him. I'm telling you this is outrageous and I'm not gonna let you be so insulted. You have rights!

Man #1

I know but let's not make a big deal outta...

Man #2

.... It's already a big deal thanks to this Sheriff of Nottingham Forest...This private impersonating a general.

Police Officer

Now wait right there!

Man #1

Yes, wait right there. Let's be the gentlemen that we are and ....

Man #2

..... And report this two-bit martinet ....

Man #1

…. Yes…. No! Just pay him the $2 and let's get out of here!

Man #2

Not a chance. He's thrown the proverbial gauntlet down. You can't cave in now. Think of all the citizens of this city whom are counting on you to stand up for them. I can't let you let them down!

Man #1

You can't?

Man #2

No you can't!

Police Officer

To Man #1…

So you're a wise guy now? We'll see about this. You're comin' with me buster and right now. Come on let's go…downtown!

Man #1

Downtown? No please not downtown!

Man #2

Don't let him intimidate you, old buddy. I'll have you bailed out by the morning.

Man #1

By the morning? Tomorrow morning? (shouting) Just pay him the $2 will ya? It's only $2 for god's sake. It's not worth going to jail!

Man #2

Oh jail's not that bad. Think of John Q Public whose rights you are protecting. Why it's a privilege to spend the night in jail for him. For all of us.

Man #1

It is?

Man #2

Sure it is. You should be proud!

Man #1

I should? Wait a minute here. I don't want the privilege. I don't even know John Q. Whoever he is. Why should I spend the night in jail for him or anybody else?

Police Officer

You don't have any choice in the matter my friend. Now get up. You're comin' with me. Let's go (He grabs Man #1 by the arm) March Buster!

Man #1

Downtown?

Police Officer

Downtown! March!

Man #2

Don't worry pal. Your name will go down in the annals of legal history. If you don't stand up for our rights, who will?

Man #1

I don't care. Pay him the $2. Please pay the $2!

Police Officer

It's too late for that Buster. Tell it to the judge. March!

They exit.

Man #2

Shouting and then following off stage.

Don't worry about a thing. I'll have you sprang by 8 a.m. Think of how proud of you the players will be.

He exits.

Lights dim. As they come back up, Man #1 is in a jail cell pacing back and forth, shivering and muttering to himself. Man #2 enters carrying his golf bag.

Man #1

Did you pay 'em the $2?

Man #2

No I did not. We're going to trial. Ever heard of Night Court?

Man #1

Night Court? Didn't you bail me out?

Man #2

I certainly tried but I refused to pay the bastards.

Man #1

Refused? How much did they want?

Man #2

$2.

Man #1

$2! Are you crazy?

Man #2

That's exactly what I asked them! $2 on a bail on a bum rap? You have no record. They should have given you personal recognizance. So why in the world would I exacerbate the injustice by paying the $2?

Man #1

Just pay 'em the $2 so I can get out of here.

Man #2

Nothing doing. You'll have the sympathy of the jury if you're locked up and brought in the court in handcuffs.

Man #1

In hand cuffs? What jury?

Man #2

You don't think we're gonna let a hanging judge who is almost certainly a former prosecutor decide your fate, do you?

Man #1

My fate?

Man #2

Sure. Your chances of acquittal are much greater with a jury.

Man #1

But there are no juries in Night Court.

Man #2

You're absolutely correct, I'm very impressed by your understanding of what you're up against. So we'll ask for adjournment until tomorrow morning.

Man #1

Tomorrow morning!

Man #2

Wednesday afternoon at the latest. Now if you'll excuse me I have a tee time in under an hour.

Man #1

Oh sure. You play golf while I stew in here like a prune. Can't you just bail me out? Pay 'em the $2. My wife is gonna kill me.

Man #2

Oh no don't worry about her. I've kept her fully informed. She sends her love. I've given her ample assurance that you will prevail on the merits so she doesn't have a thing to worry about.

Man #1

Yeah but what about me? Couldn't you pay the $2. I'm cold. I'm hungry and a couple of these guys in here are threatening me. You gotta get me out of here. Please, please pay 'em the $2.

Man #2

Oh that reminds me.

He pulls notes from his pocket.

I've got a few bills I need you to settle upon.

Man #1

Bills? What kind of bills?

Man #2

Oh just some of my expenses for handling your defense.

Man #1

What defenses? How much are they?

Man #2

Oh not much. Let's see here, $500 to Dewey, Cheetem and Howe.

Man #1

$500! What on earth for?

Man #2

Why for a second opinion of course.

Man #1

A second opinion? What did they say?

Man #2

They said pay 'em the $2.

Man #1

Totally exasperated.

What did I tell ya? That opinion cost me $500?

Man #2

Oh that's not all.

Man #1

Not all? What do ya mean that's not all?

Man #2

Well there's this bill for $150 from the technical evidence expert to determine if there was actually any spit on the cigar tip.

Man #1

What did he say?

Man #2

He said it was full of it. That you don't have a chance.

Man #1

Then that means we should pay the $2, doesn't it?

Man #2

Not exactly. He says there is no way to connect the spit to you.

Man #1

Well that's good news, isn't it?

Man #2

Yes, it certainly is. But I've got some bad news too.

Man #1

What is it?

Man #2

The dental expert can trace the bite mark on the tip to your front teeth.

Man #1

Well that's terrible!

Man #2

Not as terrible as his fee. He cost us $350! That's outrageous!

Man #1

$350!

He grabs a golf club out of the bag and threatens to clobber the attorney.

$350! That's outrageous!

Man #2

Yes, it is, and so too is your overbite!

Man #1

Why I ought to crown you! All you had to do is pay the $2. But no, you had to make a federal case out of it. Look at me. I'm miserable; shaking worried, all for what, two lousy dollars! I tell ya you're gonna be the death of me yet.

Man #2

Oh now you're being melodramatic. Think of the principle at stake here. How can you call yourself an American if you can't enjoy a leisurely smoke on a Sunday afternoon in the park? Why pretty soon we'll be saluting Joe Stalin himself unless we make a stand. I'm telling you, you are a genuine American hero!

Man #1

I don't want to be a hero. I just want to go home. Please, please, please just pay' em the $2. My health is deteriorating in here. I have a fever and the chills. I can't sleep. I've got a tick in my neck. My stomach is upset. I've gotten excruciating headaches. Just pay 'em the $2. Please!

Man #2

Oh you'll be fine. Remember what they say, if it doesn't kill you it'll make you stronger.

Man #1

But it is killing me!

Man #2

By next week you'll be laughing at the whole thing. Now if you'll excuse me, I've gotta get out to the course. I think I hear them calling my name.

He takes the golf club out of Man #1's hand and places it back in his golf bag

Man #1

The bright side? The bright side? What bright side? This whole thing has been a total catastrophe and for what, two stinkin' dollars. What bright side can you possibly be speaking about? Tell me, I've got to know! You've got me locked up for god knows how long. I'm a nervous wreck. I'm losing my hair. My legs are all swollen. I've got a rash all over my body. My vision is blurry. I've got a sinus condition, claustrophobia, a toothache and fallen arches! I'm going frickin' crazy in here! *(Shouting)* *What damn bright side are you talking about?*

Man #2

Well at least you don't have hammertoe!

He exits with a wave of his hand and a slight limp.

Man #1

Shrieks and pulls at his hair. He then kicks the jail bars and hurts his foot. He grabs it and hops around in pain.

Argh!!! I'm gonna kill you when I get outta here. If I ever get outta here. Five lousy dollars! Arghh!!!!

THE END

Three Christs
of Ypsilanti

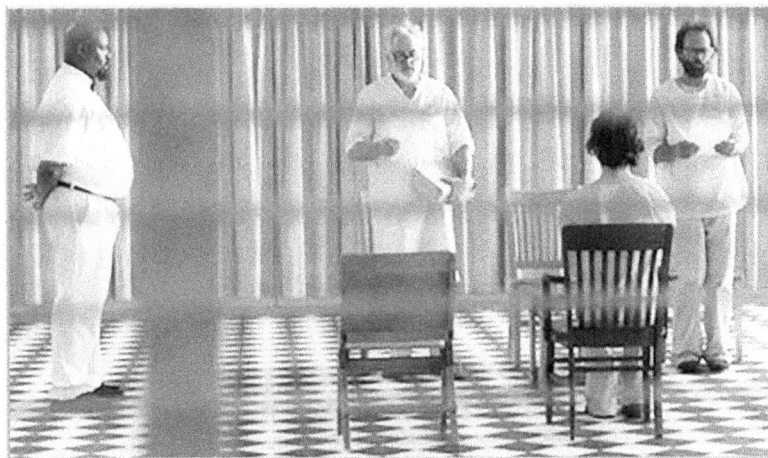

The Three Christs of Ypsilanti

**A psychiatrist explores why three mentally ill men
believe they are each Jesus Christ**

TIME: Several months in the Summer and Autumn
of 1952

SETTING: A conference room at the State Forensic Hospital, Ypsilanti, Michigan

CHARACTERS:

Frederick Bakersfield: Middle-aged male psychologist; skeptical, inquisitive, mild-mannered.

John Colvin: Age thirty-ish

Jules Dalton: Age sixty-ish

Richard Coates: Age forty-ish

*All three are patients at the above-named institution.

AT OPENING: Lights rise upon Dr. Bakersfield seated at the
head of a small conference table.

*   *   *

Bakersfield

If there is anything I can say for certain it is that my disbelief in
all things supernatural was as certain as a circle is round. To me

agnosticism is a weak man's excuse for refusing to take a stand and I'll have none of it. Either you believe or you don't because there isn't any room in between. Yes, I was comfortable in my atheism, as comfortable as any man can be about a subject so weighty. Until that day came when I was offered the opportunity to treat the Three Christs of the State Forensics Hospital for the insane in Ypsilanti. For it was then that my convictions began to falter, slowly at first to be sure. Bud in time it began to peel away in layers and all of a sudden the firm ground which I trod gave way to a feeling that I was perpetually in the hole of a ship on turbulent waters. Then one day quietly and without warning, the embrace, no the grip of Christianity seized me and reached inside me to squeeze my heart, no my soul. With the stirring the likes of which I am incapable of describing except to tell you that it was both strong and gentle, rough and soothing, and ever since then there was a kind of spur in my side so that I can now never forget the fact of my transformation or my conversion as others prefer to call it. For me it is a mystery and a mystery it shall remain. But to the Three Christs of Ypsilanti it was all in a day's work, so to speak. It all began just ten months ago. Though it seems much longer.

Lights go up.

Baker

All right, please gentlemen, you can enter now, single file mind you. That's right come in and take a seat at the table, good, very good. Now try to make yourselves comfortable. That's it, good! Now first I'd like to welcome you each: at the far end Mr. Richard Coates; in the center is Mr. John Colvin and over here we have Mr. Jules Dalton. Welcome all, gentlemen my name is Dr. Frederick Bakersfield and I'm one of the senior staff psychologists here at the hospital. Today we are going to begin…

Colvin

Interrupting…

They told me we were going to the chapel. This is not the chapel!

Baker

Now please don't interrupt me Mr. Colvin. As I was saying, today we are going to begin an interesting and I believe all together novel experiment.

Colvin

More insistent.

They told me that we were going to the chapel!

Dalton

Pipe down will ya, let the doctor speak and then I'm sure there will be plenty of time for you to have your say.

Colvin

And then go to the chapel?

Dalton

And go to the chapel, yes, now let's be charitable and open our minds and close our mouths. You were saying doctor?

Baker

Thank you Mr. Dalton.

Dalton

Sure, sure, just call me Juli.

Baker

Very well, thank you Juli, as I was saying…

Colvin

And you can call me Jesus.

Baker

Ok, Jesus, now I was saying gentlemen, please, we have much territory to cover and our time together is valuable but limited. We are going to begin small group therapy for just the three of you because each of you presents a similar, ah', challenge to those of us at the hospital there. Tell me, do any of you know or can you guess what the challenge is perceived to be?

Dalton

Well we are all in a mental hospital that must be a clue.

Baker

Don't look at me doctor, I most assuredly don't belong in here.

Baker

In the hospital?

Colvin

No, in this room. I was told that we were going to the chapel.

Baker

I promise you Mr. Colvin, as soon as we are finished with today's session you can go to the chapel. I promise, okay?

Colvin

They all make me promises around here and seldom are they ever kept.

Baker

I will escort you to the chapel myself Mr. Colvin. Is that sufficient?

Colvin

Seeing is believing.

Coates

Not always, faith is not a matter of sight but of conviction. "For no man proceedeth to the father except through me."

Dalton

I beg your pardon gentlemen. Through me!

Baker

Okay, let's not get ahead of ourselves, simmer down all of you. But now you've broken my egg, so to speak. That's why each of you are here.

Coates

Why?

Dalton

Yes, please explain why.

Colvin

You certainly better because you're keeping me from the chapel.

Baker

Because gentlemen each of you is suffering from a, umm, similar malady and it is my hope that by speaking to you collectively we might arrive at some common conclusions as to both pathology and treatment. Do each of you understand?

Coates

I only understand one thing doctor; the Son of Man is the Lamb of God who is come to taketh away the sins of the world. I and my father are one.

Dalton

Exactly so!

Baker

And each of you claim to be, ah, Jesus Christ.

Colvin

The Savior!

Dalton

Exactly so!

Baker

But one of you perhaps, certainly not all three of you.

Colvin

Ever heard of the Trinity doctor?

He starts to laugh and the other two join in. Even Jesus is not without his mirth.

Dalton

That is correct!

Coates

I quite agree with you Juli although in truth there is nothing amusing about the Trinity, we are one in substance, separate but undivided.

Dalton

Hear, hear, well said, Mr. Coates.

Coates

You can call me Jesus.

Dalton

But I prefer to address you by your surname all the same.

Coates

As you wish, Juli.

Dalton nods courteously.

Baker

Gentlemen I'm delighted at the civil tone. Shall we agree to be respectful even if we disagree? But tell me Mr. Colvin, how do you feel that Mr. Coates and Mr. Dalton have claimed your identity?

Colvin

It means nothing at all to me because anybody can tell they are mere imposters.

Baker

Mr. Coates, what do you say to that? Is it the truth, is Mr. Colvin the only Christ?

Coates

Many will come in my name…

Dalton

And mine!

Coates

… but few will walk in the shadow of the almighty…

Dalton

… Or do his works as he commands.

Colvin

May I remind you gentlemen; even the Devil will quote scripture for his purpose.

The others look at him with severity.

Colvin

It's the highest form of flattery.

Coates

Let me ask you a question; how would you react if someone else claimed to be Dr. Frederick Bakersfield?

Baker

I wouldn't believe him.

Coates

And there you have my answer.

Dalton

And mine.

Baker

So would you feel the same way Juli?

Dalton

It doesn't lessen the truth a tad. Calling a pear tree an apple tree doesn't make it so, does it doctor? A pear is still a pear no matter what you call it.

Baker

Well said Juli, well said. Do you agree Mr. Colvin?

Colvin

To a point I suppose but we could settle the dispute here and now with a simple demonstration. Only the anointed one can perform miracles. Ask each of these fellows to perform a miracle and you'll have your proof soon enough.

Baker

Good idea Mr. Colvin. But why don't you show us a miracle of your own making first. As a kind of good will gesture. After all Jesus was nothing if not magnanimous.

Colvin

Now you don't think I'm going to fall for that trick do you doctor? If Satan can't tempt me what makes you believe you can? Come come doctor: It was you who spoke of civility.

Baker

Forgive me Mr. Colvin, I can assure you no trick was intended. After all, it was you who proposed that miracles would be proof enough of who is really Christ and who is not.

Colvin

I don't need to prove anything to anybody. I am Truth, The Way and The Light.

Baker

Very well, as you wish. Tell me Mr. Dalton, Juli, would you be willing to perform a miracle to settle the question?

Dalton

Certainly not; to do so would debase the glory of the Father. Miracles are a result of deep faith doctor. Those who feed on the Lord's love find the faith they need and no miracle is a substitute for that love. "Seek first the Kingdom of God and his Righteousness and all things shall be added to you" Matthew: 6:32-33.

Baker

Mr. Coates, what do you say to that?

Coates

"The things which are impossible to men are possible with God," Luke: 18:27.

Baker

No, I mean to the suggestion that the performance of a miracle might settle the question.

Coates

Miracles by the Grace of God are not like magic tricks doctor. Any amateur can pull a rabbit out of a hat but only the Son of Man, acting on behalf of the Father and only with his blessing can perform a miracle. So the suggestion is a sound one but the conditions are not conducive. I must therefore decline.

Baker

Very well, perhaps it wasn't such a good idea in the first place. But, do you believe that quoting from the Bible, as each of you have done thus far, is convincing Mr. Colvin?

Colvin

I wasn't aware I needed to convince you of anything Doctor Bakersfield. I believe you are the one requiring the convincing.

Baker

Oh really, why do you say that?

Colvin

Because it's obvious that's why.

Baker

What, that I need convincing that you are Christ?

Colvin

No, no I don't care about your opinion on that subject. I'm speaking about your lack of conviction that the Almighty reigns from his kingdom. The fundamental belief, that there is a God in heaven and that he sent his only begotten son - me - to this world to save mankind from eternal death.

Coates

Close but I would put it slightly different. That he sent his only begotten son - me - to cleanse away the sins of the world so that mankind, by receiving his blessing by faith should have life everlasting in heaven.

Colvin

Same difference.

Dalton

Yes, I agree same difference. The exact words are not important; it is the love of our Lord that matters. To do that one must be truly repentant for his sins, meaning one must turn away from this world. The only way to do this, according to the Word, is to accept me, Christ, into your heart as the only means of salvation, for no man shall gain the Kingdom of God except through me.

Colvin

Through me!

Coates

Through me!

Baker

You must be a Baptist.

Dalton

I am the way.

Coates

I am the truth.

Colvin

And I am the light. May I go to the chapel now doctor?

Baker

Okay, gentlemen, let's call it a day. Same time tomorrow, shall we?

Lights dim to dark, after a moment they rise again.

Baker

Greetings gentlemen, I trust you have each given thought to our first session yesterday. I was enlightened by it to say the least, and by the way, I apologize that I neglected to inform you that I am tape recording these sessions so that I can listen to them afterwards and make notes. That's why you don't see me taking notes here. Do I have each of your permission to record our sessions? You can decline of course.

Colvin

But you'd do it anyway so what is the use.

Baker

No, you are wrong I wouldn't record without the consent of all. You see, establishing complete trust is the key to successful treatment. Psychotherapy can never be meaningful if it is not honest and sincerely conducted. Do each of you understand?

They all nod.

Okay, I thank you. Now, having said that, and after reviewing our first session audio tapes, I was struck by two things. The first is the level of candor, which I thought was very good considering this is just our second session. I thank you each for that. It demonstrates a level of trust among us. But the second thing I was struck by is more revealing. We know Christ to be a man of humility he is described as the Lamb of God and as The Servant of Man. Yet I detected a noticeable air of pride, if not self-righteousness, in each of your statements. I thought that was quite puzzling. You could say it's ironic. Mr. Coates, what do you say to that?

Coates remains silent and motionless.

Mr. Coates are you listening to me? Are you going to participate today? Mr. Coates?

He appears to ignore the doctor by staring straight ahead.

Very well, have it your way. What about you Mr. Dalton, Juli?

Dalton

Can you repeat the question?

Baker

Certainly, I detected a certain lack of humbleness, if I can use that word - if it is a word - but you know what I mean - humility in each of your remarks yesterday. Don't you see that as un-Christ like?

Dalton

Ah yea. If I appear the least bit forward I regret it is no way for the Savior to act, especially to a Psychiatrist. I apologize and if I gave offense to you gentlemen then I apologize to each of you as well.

Colvin

Don't you think it is obvious doctor, I mean what would you expect if you challenge someone's identity by placing two others around him who claim it? Wouldn't you expect anyone, even Jesus Christ, to become defensive? After all, on earth Jesus is but a man.

Dalton

But not without his divine return.

Colvin

Yes of course, but a man nevertheless.

Baker

So, you are saying that a kind of competition is present and as a result the ego emerges to assist identity. Is that right?

Colvin

I cannot speak of the ego. If there's anything Christ lacks it is an ego.

Dalton

I subscribe to that statement. Humility is the opposite of ego.

Baker

What about you Mr. Coates? What do you think?

Coates

Yesterday I asked you to call me Jesus. Yet you specifically ignored this request.

Baker

Yes, I did but only in respect of Mr. Colvin and Mr. Dalton because I thought that they might object.

Colvin

Not me, I have no objection. He can ask to be called anything he wishes. It doesn't lessen my sense of certainty one iota.

Baker

Okay, what about you Mr. Dalton?

Dalton

I believe it would be inappropriate. Under the circumstances surnames shall be utilized.

Coates

1st John second chapter verses 22 & 23 among others emphasize that many imposters will emerge but only one is empowered by the Almighty.

Baker

I'm glad that you brought that up; it's something I wish to explore. If Jesus in fact warned us against being fooled by imposters, aren't each of you suspect? After all, my reading of the book of Revelations tells me His second coming will be a cataclysmic event and signal the end of the world as we know it.

Colvin

Not at all doctor, like many you misinterpret the Word.

Dalton

Yes, you misinterpret the Word.

Baker

Okay, who would care to set me straight? Anybody?

All are silent.

I find this silence a little surprising.

Coates

When the end times commence my Father will send me to signify the final triumph of good over evil. Until then, the Father has planted The Son of Man amid the living to be a witness to all that is wicked and unholy.

Dalton

Yes, I agree with that, very true.

Baker

I've noticed that you are a very agreeable figure Mr. Dalton. I wonder are you afraid to disagree or assert yourself in some contrary way?

Dalton

I don't believe so. God whispers to me, he says I shall always be gentle and loving.

Baker

Is that how God communicates with you Mr. Colvin, by whispering to you?

Colvin

It's varied, but yes, sometimes it is by whispering. Other times he gives me notes.

Baker

Leaves you notes? May I see one?

Colvin

Certainly not, besides you wouldn't be able to read them anyway. The Lord has his own kind of shorthand. Not being inspired, you wouldn't be able to understand it.

Baker

I see but can you show me one even if I can't read it. I could at least see it. I'd very much like to see God's penmanship and to hold a paper sent from him. I don't presume they came in the mail do they?

Colvin

As a matter of fact, they do.

Baker

They do? Does God have to purchase postage stamps? That's very odd.

Colvin

The Lord can do anything and so it is never odd.

Dalton

I agree.

Coates

I believe you are missing the point doctor. All things are possible with the Father.

Lights dim on the patients but remain on Bakersfield. He addresses the audience.

Baker

And thus we proceed week after week. I must confess I didn't believe we were getting anywhere. Now mind you I was not losing patience with my patients. Frankly I was continually fascinated by them. Neither of them ever budged off their claims, in fact, I noticed as went along their resolve actually strengthened. It's as if speaking about their delusions fortified them. And what always struck me as so peculiar about it all is how very different each of them are from one another. They are all psychotic without question but only one of them has actually been proven to be dangerous. The other two are quite passive and well-behaved. I put them through a battery of tests. The results were both interesting and predictable. They don't agree on anything and I mean anything except that they are each the living embodiment of Christ. And interestingly, none of them seems the least bit alarmed that at least two others claim his identity. I find that very puzzling. They do not appear to be in the least bit insecure in their belief of who they are. Oh yes, and I should add that none of them exhibit the typical symptoms of schizophrenia. Again, very puzzling.

Lights up.

Baker

Okay gentlemen, we are now in our fourteenth week. You know we started the same time as the Presidential Campaign started. And now it's almost election time. Tell me Mr. Coates, who do you support?

Coates

I favor Harry Truman but since he's not running again I support the Democratic Candidate Mr. Stevenson. I was born in Illinois so I support a fellow Illinoisan.

Baker

Okay, good, what about you Mr. Colvin, who do you support?

Colvin

I don't like either and don't plan on voting.

Baker

Why not, didn't Christ say "render unto Caesar that which is Caesar's."

Coates

And unto God that which is God's!

Colvin

Yes, I know, I know but Eisenhower is a dunce and Stevenson is a pinhead. The only person worth voting for is Nixon. Now there's an honest man!

Baker

Okay and you Mr. Dalton, what's your opinion?

Dalton

I'm going to vote for General Eisenhower. If they let us vote that is. I witnessed the carnage of Omaha Beach firsthand.

Baker

Oh yes, you all can vote. The administration thinks it's a good idea for all p patients and is arranging to get that organized with the County Clerk. Of course you have to be a registered voter. Are all of you registered?

All remain silent.

Have any of you ever voted before?

They each shake their heads.

Well then, this will be a good time to start even if we have our own election. We'll render unto Caesar. Okay gentlemen, now I'd like to change directions for today's session. We've spent a great deal of time together but I realized last night when I was reviewing the tapes that we haven't learned as much as we should about your personal histories, and I consider myself remiss in this regard. So this afternoon I'd like to pierce the veil and find out more about each of you, and importantly I believe it will be helpful for each of you to learn more about each other. Is that acceptable to all of you? Do any of you have any objections to sharing this kind of information?

Colvin

Exactly what kind of information are you thinking about?

Dalton

I think we should maintain some boundaries.

Baker

I agree, but if you chose not to share anything then your wishes will be respected.

Coates

I and the Father are one, that's all you need to know about me.

Baker

Pauses.

Do you wish to elaborate on that claim Mr. Coates?

Coates

Not really, it's very clear.

Baker

Tell us about your biological father.

Coates

His name is Joseph. He died when I was in High School.

Baker

Was he a carpenter?

Coates

Indeed, He was!

Baker

Tell me, did you resemble him in any way? Your receding hair-line for example, did you inherit it from him? Or your eye color? Was he about your height and weight? Tell us about those kinds of traits.

Colvin

Don't answer that, it's a trick question! Come, come doctor, do you think we are idiots?

Dalton

Yes, I agree. Do you think we are fools?

Baker

Not at all. It's a straight-forward question. Surely all of us inherit traits from our biological parents. Were any of you born from a virgin? Do any of you have any older brothers or sisters?

All are silent.

What about you Mr. Coates, was your mother a virgin when she gave birth to you?

Coates

Indeed, she was!

Baker

What about you Mr. Dalton?

Dalton

Yes, of course she was, have you ever heard of Immaculate Conception?

Colvin

Of course he hasn't. Haven't you realized all along that our inquisitor is an Atheist? Or maybe he's just a lapsed Catholic. In which case he's heard of it but has forgotten what it signifies, otherwise he wouldn't have asked such an idiotic question.

Dalton

Yes, you are probably correct.

Baker

Ah huh. But at least two of you have an older sibling; does that strike you as odd? How could a virgin have given birth prior to you? Unless your older brother and sister were also immaculately conceived.

Coates

It seems obvious then that virginity is not a pre-condition to Immaculate Conception.

Colvin

Frankly I resent receiving treatment from an Atheist.

Dalton

I do too!

Baker

What about you Mr. Coates, do you resent being treated by a non-believer?

Coates

Not at all. The Father sent me to save sinners and those who are lost like the sheep and the Prodigal Son.

Baker

Sinners like me?

Coates

If you do not accept his word and obey his commandments, sinners like you and everyone else. We are saved by Grace and it is a gift from God lest any man should boast.

Baker

I can see that Mr. Colvin obviously reads the Bible because he always carries it with him and it looks well-worn from use. And Mr. Coates, I've noticed you often quote from the Bible so I presume you are well versed in it well.

Coates

I am.

Baker

Tell me Mr. Dalton, do you read the Bible too?

Dalton

I know it by heart.

Baker

Can you recite the Ten Commandments for me?

Dalton

Of course!

Baker

Can you two as well?

Coates

Yes, would you like me to?

Baker

If you wish you may.

Colvin

I can recite the names of the Seven Dwarfs too doctor, but what does that prove?

Baker

Now I don't believe you.

Colvin

Testing me are you? Doc, Grumpy, Sneezy, Sleepy, Dopey, Bashful, Happy. There can I go now?

Baker

Not just yet. Can you name the Seven Wonders of the Ancient World?

Colvin

Ask me something difficult doctor.

Baker

Okay, what is the meaning of life?

Colvin

That's not difficult.

Baker

No?

Dalton

I agree.

Baker

Than tell them what is it? The meaning of life?

Colvin

Pauses.

To love our Lord - your God with all your heart, mind, and soul and to love your neighbor as you love yourself - Matthew 22:37-39.

Baker

And then love gives life its meaning?

Colvin

Of course it does.

Baker

Do you agree Mr. Coates? I know you do Mr. Dalton.

Dalton

Yes, it's a good answer and I do agree.

Baker

Can you amplify it for us?

Coates

Man was created in the image of God.

Baker

In his physical image?

Coates

No, no of course not, in his spirit, his image is in spirit.

Baker

I see, Okay I'm sorry to interrupt you, please continue.

Coates

Thus man was meant to live in communion with the Father and to be seated upon his throne. After all, we are all Christ in that we are children of the Father.

Dalton

Exactly!

Coates

But man was separated from God by sin. I was sent to redeem man's sin. Thus the meaning of life is to restore man's bond with the Father.

Baker

Mr. Dalton would you care to comment beyond signaling your assent?

Dalton

Certainly, life is made meaningful by forgiveness and we have that by the gift of love and sacrifice. Man is forgiven, that is his gift.

Forgiveness cannot be earned, lest man should boast or believe good deeds will open the gates of the kingdom.

Baker

And the meaning of life is?

Dalton

That mankind should recognize and accept the gift of forgiveness of sin. We accomplish this by the act of atonement.

Baker

That is most profound.

Colvin

Dalton, Coates, I must admit you've nailed it, no pun intended.

He laughs.

And the other two join in, first Dalton and then Coates. As they laugh together heartily, and joyfully, the lights above them gradually diminish. The spot targets Bakersfield similar to how it shone upon him at the start.

Bakersfield

And so our sessions continued. I readily confess, nothing in my medical training or clinical experience prepared me for what was essentially a litany of religious and philosophical discussions and challenges. And I confess to also feeling a measure of shame - no of guilt - that I learned more from our sessions than they appear to have learned. Two years have passed. I've started writing a book about our experiences together. I've shared my findings with my colleagues and have published a paper on this process in a prestigious journal. I've been invited to give a lecture next month at the annual meeting of the American Psychiatric Association. But the transformation I had hoped to achieve, maybe transcendence is a more appropriate word, failed to occur in the Three Christs, who remain virtually unchanged after all this treatment. No, the transformation has occurred in me! And I have these three remarkable men to thank for it. Amen to that!

The lights above the Three Christs return and they continue laughing.

THE END

Nowhere Man

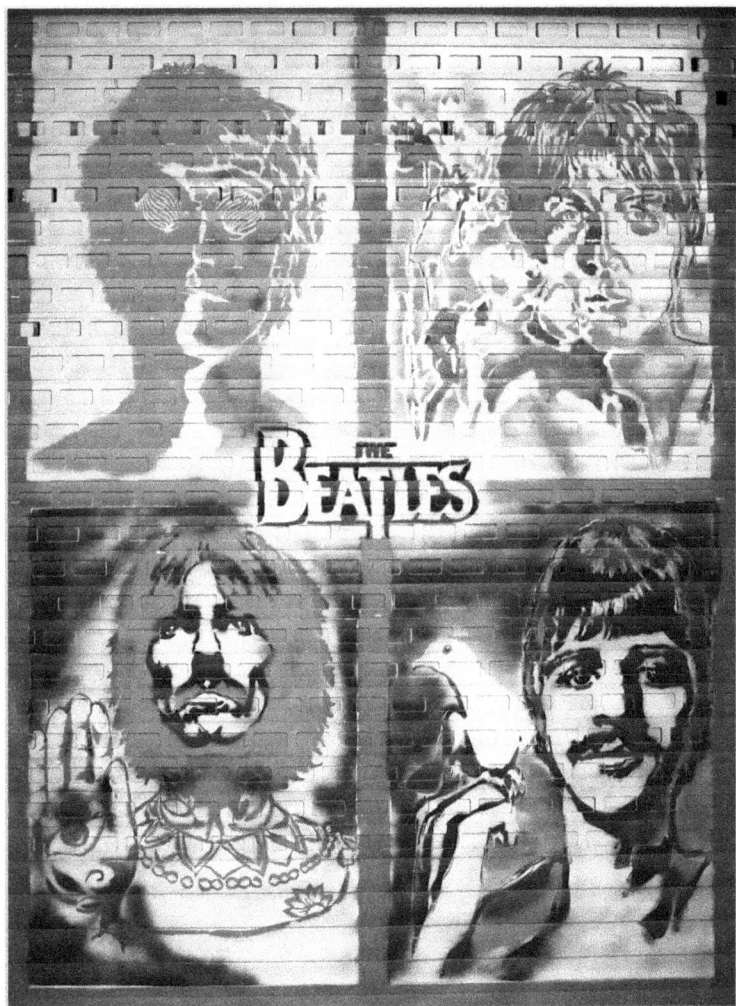

Nowhere Man

Alf Bicknell recalls his years working for and with The Beatles

Preface

This one-man play script was written for a gentleman named George Alfred "Alf" Bicknell, who passed away suddenly in 2008 at his home in Oxfordshire, England. I believe he was about 76 years old. He was a kind and jolly fellow, looking like Santa Claus, and I enjoyed our conversations together, which occurred in 2005 over a period of three months. It's my one, very remote, connection to The Beatles, a band that I always admired and whose story I was always fascinated by. This project permitted me to dive deep into that story and revisit things I knew and learn much that I did not.

Alf had the distinction of working as the exclusive driver and gofer/assistant to The Beatles from March 1964 (just after their return from their first visit to the United States, where they famously performed on The Ed Sullivan Show) until the autumn of 1966, when he decided he had had enough of the craziness of those Fab Four years. For about a year prior to his departure from their employ, Alf and his wife resided in a house on the grounds of John and Cynthia Lennon's estate called Tittenhurst Park. Naturally they were very close.

When Alf decided to move up to Oxford, John and him spent a day sorting through the garage and emptying the contents of John's famous Rolls Royce (later painted in psychedelic swirls). When I first met Alf he was in need of cash and decided to finally sell all the memorabilia John had given him and that he otherwise collected during his time with The Beatles. I knew an actor who knew a fellow who knew Alf, and this acquaintance contacted me and asked me if I knew anybody who might be interested in acquiring Alf's memorabilia collection. It just so happened, I did know a vintage rock and roll dealer who had recently opened a store on Ebay, which was new to me back then. To make a long story short, Alf came to the United States with his collection and I met him with the dealer in Orlando, Florida. As he showed us the items he brought with him (all the while explaining he had much more at home) I was greatly impressed, dazzled even, knowing many of the items were given to him by Lennon himself. There was a bag of fan mail letters that had been opened but never responded to. There was an autographed blue vinyl BOAC airlines travel bag. There was a chauffer's cap he told us that John asked him not to wear any longer because he thought it too servile. There was also a wide variety Beatles toys, accessories and other licensed products which fans had sent in asking that it be signed and returned. Obviously it never was. And I remember a box of mini reel-to-reel tapes that fans, mostly teen girls, recorded and mailed to The Beatles to gush about their love for them and their music. Remember, this was in the early days when Beatlemania was wild and rampant. In all there were about three hundred items that we inspected and pawed.

At dinner that evening, Alf shared with me his desire to give talks in the states about his recollections of his years at The Beatles' sides. He said he had many great memories and told me stories that he had compiled in a limited-edition book he titled Baby You Can Drive My Car and said Paul McCartney told him that Alf's driving skills inspired him to write that song. Before we said good bye that night, I had agreed to write Alf's presentation and he agreed to try to memorize it.

Being a theatre nerd, I come up with a one-man play rather than a "talk" as he wanted to do. I told him my years of experience in Edinburgh and London had convinced me that one-person shows were all the rage and could get him better bookings and earn him more income than what he had envisioned for himself. Due to the fact that we met while he was showing us his memorabilia, I decided to let that serve as the narrative framework for the show. He liked that idea and it seemed to work very well. So we went over a list of items I asked him to withhold from his planned sale and we agreed to place those things in a prop box to use for the show. He was most agreeable to all my suggestions and I enjoyed his company very much. Alf was a big fellow and with his long white her and beard, and hearty laugh, he had a lot of Santa Claus about him. How can you not like that?

When we conversed, I paid special attention to Alf's tone, diction and style of speaking. I wanted to make his voice as authentic as I could muster. Alf's English accent was not irregular or uncommon so I wasn't faced with the task of repeating a lot of off-beat vernacular that might not be easily comprehended by an American audience. He was kindly, even-tempered and formal and I thought it was best to maintain that style though out his monologue. So, if the reader perceives it to be a little too formal, that's just me trying to be faithful to Alf's voice.

But alas, our hopes to perform this show never materialized due to Alf's sudden death. I well remember when I heard the sad news. I had hired another actor friend of mine named Benji Ming, who also lived in Oxford (like so many others, on a canal boat), to act as his dramaturg and then as   a director to work with Alf on polishing his delivery. Alf was no actor but he wanted to do a good job, so he was very easy to work with. But I think it may have been too much for him. He became worried about my approach and he wondered if the travel schedule I was arranging for him would be too much for him to handle. And he had trouble memorizing what became a very long script. I did my best to reassure him and his apprehensions about the forthcoming tour I arranged for him seemed manageable. I could thank Benji, our interlocutor, for that. And so it was in a phone call from Benji that I heard of Alf's death. He told me that Alf had a heart attack while sitting at his breakfast table, the script sprawled out next to his cold toast and coffee mug.

So Alf's project died with Alf. I thought about reviving it with another actor but then, it wouldn't be the same. Alf was the Real McCoy. He was the Nowhere Man of the title. A proverbial fly on the wall of The Beatles' mid-career period, when they exploded all bounds of popular fame. But the ironic thing about the whole story is simply this: Alf's assignment as The Beatles' chauffer began as a serendipitous event. He just happened to be in the right place at the right time. Beatles' manager Brian Epstein had summarily fired their previous chauffer when he spoke without authorization to the ever-pestering press. Epstein believed the man accepted a fee for gossip and this he would not tolerate. So when The Beatles needed a ride to a photography studio, a call was placed to a car service and Alf just happened to be the next name on the list. Call it luck because that's just wat it was. Truth is stranger than fiction, that's for sure.

R.I.P. Alf. Thanks for the stories and laughter.

At Opening:

The stage has a single box upon it. As pre-show music fades, lights dim except for a single spotlight over the box, which slowly fades out. Darkness. The spotlight slowly resumes again to reveal the box lid is now opened. An offstage voice is heard:

> Ladies and Gentlemen, welcome to each of you. My name is George Alfred Bicknell but everyone always just called me Alf. I'm going to tell you a story, a long story no doubt but one which is made somewhat shorter by pure enchantment. It's the story of how these four lads became these for men.

First and last photos of The Beatles flash on a projection screen. Lights go up on Alf.

*   *   *

Alf:

Though I worked closely with The Beatles for two and a half years, all during the very height of Beatlemania, I was not fond of telling stories about them. I pretty much kept it all to myself. You see, to me The Beatles were always like family. And I am not one to talk badly or evenly openly about my family. Not like some I imagine. So I kept it to myself.

But about fifteen years ago I went to see Paul McCartney in concert in Birmingham and it brought back a rush of memories as powerful to me as Niagara Falls. Then I stumbled upon this box here, which I hadn't seen in perhaps twenty-five years. I thought it was lost and I had long gotten over its loss. It turns out I had it all along, it was just hiding in another, bigger box. When I moved from North Wales to Oxford, I found it, and it didn't have a speck of dust on top because of the way it was hidden away, in another box that I thought just contained old sweaters and socks or something.

Then I heard something about something called eBay. It got me thinking. So, one day I opened it up and took a look at what was inside. Now believe it or not, this was not an easy thing for me to do. I'm not sure if I can describe it but it was as if some strange force kept me from going there. It's not that I didn't want to go back there, to the mid 1960's, it's just that I found it hard to take the first step because I knew it would be a long and emotional journey. By nature, I'm just not a very sentimental fellow. So, the box sat there for weeks, haunting me like a ghost from another lifetime.

But once I determined to do it, I did so without trepidation, and frankly, I haven't been the same since. I didn't remember how much I had forgotten.

Now let me tell you about how this box came to be. It was October 1966 and The Beatles and I had just returned from their final tour of the US. It was a hellish tour and we were so happy to be back at home in London, safe and quiet. Relatively speaking of course. For The Beatles there was really no such thing as calm and peaceful. There were just periods of   quiet that punctuated even greater periods of screaming, hysteria, laughter, tumult, rushing around and general all-around craziness. Up to that time I had spent almost every day for the past two and a half years working for The Beatles and being with all or each of them, first as their personal chauffer and then as their bodyguard, gopher, roadie, assistant and in time, as their true and loyal friend.

But when they decided to end their touring and live performances because it all became just to crazy, I decided to walk away from it all myself. It was like a long roller coaster ride. Lots of fun and lots of thrills but in time it became a bit too chaotic for me, as for all of us. Actually, that's an understatement if there ever was one. It was just nuts and I figured I had my fill. Just like a bowl of nuts.

So here I am all alone with John Lennon in his garage at his home in Weybridge, south of London. We were both finally feeling rested from our travels. It was like that after a Beatles tour. After so much noise and hype, it was good to come back down to earth and everybody always took a few weeks off from the grind. Since I had handed in my resignation, I asked John if I could bring his car around to sort of symbolically turn it back over to him. At that time Jean, my wife, and our son Mark and I were living in a small cottage on the grounds of his estate. Then he called me one afternoon early that October and said he was ready to see me.

This box was in the garage and John and I began to sort through all of the junk that was in the trunk, the boot we say, and everything he gave me was tossed into the box. I took it home and for a period of a couple of weeks, sorted through my own things and put them in the box. After that I moved on and it got misplaced, no, forgotten, until I found it a few years ago after my move. It's really just that simple.

So shall we have a look inside? Okay, lets.

Alf takes a seat and sits beside the box.

You know, it's amazing at how many people collect Beatles memorabilia. Once I surfaced from beneath the woodwork of time, I got tons of inquiries from people all over asking if I had this or that for sale. That's why finding this box was such a delight for me. I wanted to know what I had too since I really hadn't remembered. Like I said, it was like another lifetime ago to me. Like George sang in that song about John, "All those years ago." I knew exactly what he meant. It was all such a long time ago, but in some respects, oddly enough, I remember some things as if they were just yesterday. And when I finally opened the box and took a look inside, the memories burst back one by one, like apples falling from a tree.
Mind you, I have not placed these things, these mementos, in any particular order so don't expect me to tell my tale in chronologic order. But I'll do my best to give you the context in which they originated so you'll be able to achieve some understanding of the events I'm about to relate.

Alf opens the box and looks into it for a moment. He then pulls out the first item.

Right, this is as good as any place to start.

Item One—A notebook

This notebook is my sorry attempt at writing a diary. When I was first asked to join The Beatles as their driver, they were pretty suspicious of just about everybody getting close to them. And you really couldn't get much closer to them than as their driver because way back then they were always together, just the four of them. Now it is important for you to note that in the beginning of their careers as pop stars, The Beatles were totally unprepared for the swiftness of their rise to fame, and of the level of their success and popularity. They were four very young men from working class families in Liverpool. It is safe to say they were completely unprepared for their success and at that early time, back in 1964 when they exploded onto the world stage, they were really loving it.

In the summer and autumn of 1963 they had become the biggest thing ever in British music, with hits like *Love Me Do, Please Please Me, Twist and Shout, All My Loving,* and *She Loves You.* One after the other, all number ones. They appeared on television and on the radio and they toured around the country playing at first back-up to well-known singers and then, quite suddenly, as headliners in their own right. They personified a sound that was immediately labeled The Mersey Beat, taking the name of the river that ran through Liverpool to the ocean, The Mersey. Everyone remembers that famous old hit *Ferry Across the Mersey* by Gerry Marsden and the Pacemakers...well they were from Liverpool too, as were a host of other bands Derry and the Seniors, Cass and the Casanovas, Gordon Bell and the Bobby Bell Rockers, Faron and the Flamingos, the Swinging Blue Jeans, Lee Curtiss and the All-Stars and of course, the biggest of them all, Rory Strom and the Hurricanes, which was Ringo's first band. In the early days, I'm talking about 1961 and 1962

The Beatles and a number of other Mersey Beat bands played the clubs in Hamburg, West Germany. That's where John, Paul and George met Ringo, when he was with Rory Storm, who was like a Liverpudlian Elvis except he was tall and thin and wore his blonde hair all combed up and around like a great bouffant. Rory also wore bright colored suits and black boots and moved his body like a slinky. Of course the girls loved him. And so too did The Beatles, who at that time featured a fellow named Pete Best on drums. Pete was a local chap whose mother opened a teenager music club in her house cellar just so she could keep an eye on Pete and his brothers. Liverpool at that time was a tough place and parents were wise to keep a leash on their kids. That club was called The Casbah. It was a neat hang out with murals, posters and cast-off pieces of mismatched furniture and one of the first places The Beatles had an opportunity to sing and play for people. This is long before the Cavern Club and the trips to Hamburg, mind you.

Anyway, on October 13, 1963 The Beatles rocketed onto the national stage with a live performance on the popular television music show, *Val Parnell's Sunday Night at the London Palladium*. They were an immediate sensation. And not just in England but across Europe. So much so that they were invited to play a few shows in Sweden. When they returned at the end of October, Beatlemania had begun. That's the first time thousands of fans gathered at the airport to welcome them home, with their hand-lettered banners and never ending screams for attention. It was a sign of things to come.

Once home they embarked upon a tour of England and then appeared at the Royal Command Performance at the Prince of Wales Theater before an audience which included the cream of British nobility, among them, the Queen and Princess Margaret.

Prince Charles was there too. Though they were just one act on the bill, they were the headlining act. That's the occasion when John spoke to the audience and said, "Will the people in the cheaper seats clap your hands, and the rest of you can just rattle your jewelry." It's become one of the most familiar film clips of their career. And somehow, those simple words described the enormity of what had quickly transpired. Four young musicians from Liverpool had taken the country by storm. For The Beatles just coming down to London was a big thing, but to be toasted by London society was a genuine lark. There is no question they were out of their element, but for these young lads, there was no going back. It was as if a genie had escaped from a bottle and it was impossible to get her back in.

So what has all of this got to do with my diary you ask? Well, you see, I like just about everybody else in the country was amazed by the popularity and their success. The only way in which it had an impact upon me personally was when they were in town and they'd cause a snarl in traffic due to being chased by fans and with all the police and such. After all, I was a professional driver and God knows there's nothing so irksome to a chauffer or a cabbie then to get held up by congestion in streets which was really nothing more than an awful lot of nonsense. The Beatles, I mean, really. Who do they think they are? That's all I thought about them. Snappy songs of course.

Anyway, 1964 comes around and they head to America to appear on *The Ed Sullivan Show*. At that time their song *I Wanna Hold Your Hand* is number one on both the UK and US charts. Sullivan had coincidentally got a whiff of Beatlemania some months before, when he was at Heathrow Airport at the same time as The Beatles returned from Sweden. He had no idea what it was all about then, but a few short months later and they're on his show. And of course they commence to take America by storm as well. Now mind you, this is February 1964 we're talking about.

When they got back home, they started to make their first movie, *A Hard Day's Night*, by day and recorded more songs by night. Then they did a brief tour of northern England and Scotland. By this time *Can't Buy Me Love* and *Do You Want to Know a Secret* have gone to number one. In June they head off on their first world tour, playing Copenhagen, Amsterdam, then Hong Kong and then six concerts in Australia, where they were also a sensation. Everywhere they went they caused a frenzy.

When they get back home, it's to celebrate the opening of their new film, collect a few awards, make a few public appearances, write and record some more songs and BAM, they are off to America for their first tour of the states. That's when I entered the picture.

You see, as soon as he dropped them off at the airport, the driver they had been using went straight to the press and sold his story of what it was like to drive the boys around. News of this story got back to Brian Epstein, their manager and he went ballistic. It was bad enough people talking to the press, but never before had an employee of the band betrayed their confidence like this. This event caused Epstein to require everybody at NEMS, his management company to sign confidentiality agreements. This all happened immediately after their return in mid-September.

Well to make a very long story short, they needed a new driver. Somehow my name got mentioned to one of Brian's assistants, I was asked to show up for an interview at Epstein's flat in the posh Belgravia neighborhood in London. So there I went all excited at the appointed hour. I was invited into his living room and made to feel all comfortable by his house mate, a slim Black American named Lonnie. An hour passed, then another and there was no sign of the boys or Mr. Epstein. Lonnie took a phone call and asked me to stay, that they were on their way now. Another hour passed and then another, all the while Lonnie is serving me scotch and cokes and cakes and candy and such. Finally, I said, "This is silly, I've been here four hours and I'm just a working man." Lonnie apologized profusely as I left. I figured that was the last I'd ever hear from anybody connected to The Beatles. God was I wrong.

A few days later I get a call from Brian Epstein's office. It's his chief assistant, a man named Alistair Taylor. He asks me if I can get a limo in a hurry and go pick up the boys who are at a photographer's studio in Chelsea. "Sure I can," I said and so I called around to a friend in the business and I tells him, "Can I borrow your car mate, I've got to go pick up The Beatles." Sure enough, I pull up to the front of the this ordinary London building, which was the address Alistair had given me, and before I know it, swoosh, the four of them jump into the car and tell me to take them to Brian Epstein's flat. It all happened very quickly. There I was in the car with just the four of them. It was the first day of what for the next two and a half years would be the ride of a lifetime.

He holds up the notebook.

My diary, I did the best I could jotting down notes here and there, and it's a pretty good record of what I experienced by their side. I should have known better how prophetic it was all to become, I would have taken better notes. But nobody knew. Nobody could know. It was that crazy.

Let's see, what have we here?

Item Two—Photo of Alf with Ringo outside
of a hospital, Dec 1, 1964

Right, this brings up a good memory. Just before The Beatles were about to leave for their world tour in early June, Ringo came down with a case on tonsillitis. This caused him to have to miss the first few shows in Europe and he met up with them down in Australia as they were about to give their first show in Adelaide. A session drummer by the name of Jimmy Nichol was his substitute while he was in the hospital. In December, Ringo's tonsils swelled up again and he was sent to the hospital to have them removed. He was there about a week and every day I would take his wife Maureen to the hospital to visit him. I brought him books, and games and things. And lots of fan mail, which he loved to open.

When he was released there was a fan frenzy at the hospital. The press was there as always flashing pictures and trying to get a statement out of him. And there were perhaps a thousand fans in front of the hospital, blocking the street and causing your average Beatlemania mayhem. It was very much my job to protect the boys when they were in my custody. You see the police were always around, but they too would often want to touch a Beatle and ask for an autograph and such. Here I am ushering him through the crowd and getting him safely to the Austin Princess, which was the car I mostly used around town to drive them around. By this time police escorts were a necessity, and it was my job to coordinate the route being taken with them. If you weren't careful you could run over a fan or two or three, which thank God I never did, but I had a number of close calls. Including almost running over George's cats at his house one night. Anyway, that's how it was back then. Crazy but crazy good as they say. The enthusiasm for the boys was so great that it was infectious. Incidentally, you can see I was still very much the professional chauffer at the time. I was allowed to let my hair down a little later, I'll tell you about it.

One day a few weeks later, I think it was during The Beatles Christmas show at Hammersmith Odeon, I was driving the boys home after each evening's performance, which is what I did every night, even if they wanted to go to a club or somewhere else because they were always getting invites to this club or that party or wherever. Anyway, I had dropped them all off and it was just me and John in the car. It was late and we were both very tired. Suddenly, he reached towards me, grabbed off my chaffer cap and tossed it out the window, "You didn't need this anymore, Alf, you're one of us now."

I didn't think about it then, but I'm sure it must have hit John then and there that here he was, a working-class lad from Liverpool being chauffeured in limo by a manservant or sorts. It must have offended his sense of propriety. He didn't like the idea of playing the role of the successful celebrity or the rich English gentleman. Getting rid of my black cap was probably just his small way or reclaiming some of his sanity. Because to all of us near to them, working with The Beatles was nothing if not insane. I'd show you the cap but of course it was tossed out the car window. I wonder who has it now? If they only knew.

Okay, what's next?

Item Three—A photograph of the band in the studio

Yes, there is a good story here, another long one I'm afraid. Here we are at EMI studio number two of the famed Abbey Road. It's impossible for me to remember which day this was or which session.

The fact is that I was with The Beatles while they recorded their magic on what seems like hundreds of occasions. There really isn't much to tell actually. It was always pretty much the same. Usually, I'd pick each of them up in the afternoon, after lunch, and drive them to Abbey Road for a session that would end late at night. At nine or ten at night I'd pop off to a small Italian restaurant and bring back a spread of food and wine. They'd all take a break, they meaning the boys, their producer George Martin, their engineer Norman Smith, a technician or two and of course, their two closest associates, Neil Aspinal and Mal Evans. Nobody was closer to or served The Beatles longer than Neil and Mal. For the entire length of my service in their employ, Neil, Mal and I were the closest people to the boys, except their families of course. But I'll tell you this, we spent more time with them than their own families, which is a testament to the enormous amount of work they did. All the time I was with the boys it was non-stop. That was especially true in the studio.

For the most part, when I wasn't attending to their meals or checking with the security officers out front, I was playing cards or chess with Neil. Mal was usually busy with the boysa terrible end. And to make it even worse, John paid for his cremation in the studio fixing their guitars and all that kind of things. He was the technical one, their first real roadie. God Bless his soul, he was killed by the LA police in 1976 while he was high and out of control. The cops were called to his apartment because his girlfriend called them and told them how was beating her up. When they arrived, according to the police report, Mal refused to surrender. They went into his bedroom where, they say, he had a gun and he was simply blown away. Good old Mal Evans. Everyone was shocked that he met such but the ashes were lost in the mail.

But back to the studio where Mal was very much alive and a close collaborator in The Beatles evolving sounds. Here was Neil and I, sitting outside the studio watching the boys as they developed their songs. I paid close attention to them because I wanted to see how they worked. And usually it was the same. Whoever wrote the song pretty much figured out how it went and the others, along with George Martin, figured out how to play it and record it. I have vivid memories of many particular evenings at studio number 2. It's not really important that I describe them. Let me just tell you this, to give you an idea. Over those two and a half years they recorded some of their greatest songs, and I was there to witness it. A great privilege indeed. I can recall songs like *I Feel Fine, We Can Work It Out, Yesterday, Ticket to Ride, Nowhere Man, Hello Goodbye, Michelle, You've Got to Hide Your Love Away, Baby You Can Drive My Car* (which I never ever fancied had always been written about me), *Eleanor Rigby, Eight Days A Week, Help, I'm A Loser, The Night Before, You're Gonna Lose That Girl, Day Tripper, In My Life, Taxman, Paperback Writer, Rain, Got to Get You Into My Life, All Too Much, Act Naturally, With a Little Help From My Friends, Here There and Everywhere, Good Day Sunshine,* and so many others. God knows you know them all. It was really fantastic. Who would have ever thought Lennon and McCartney had so many brilliant songs in them?

I was actually involved in the creation of two songs, all be it, in a very small way. Once I was asked by John to hold up an envelope which had some song lyrics on it. They were written all around and, in a jumble, and I couldn't for the life of me make it out. To be honest I don't remember the name of that song or if it was ever even released. All I remember is John motioning me with his head and his eyes and then in frustration saying, "Okay Alfie, that's enough, you can get lost now." Just like John. If there was ever anybody with a cruel tongue it was John Lennon. Just one of the many facets of his intriguing character.

The other time I had more direct input. This was during the recording of *Yellow Submarine*. I remember the session going on forever and we were all a bit giddy. George Martin had this idea for a chorus at the end, because, after all, it was for an animated movie that was being made in America and The Beatles didn't really have much to do with it. But they did agree to record a handful of new songs to support it. It was late and it was the last song and everyone wanted to get the hell out of there and so everyone at the studio that night was asked to sing along, you know the part "We all live in a yellow submarine, a yellow submarine, a yellow submarine," etc. Well one of those voices is mine. And I also found a chain and a metal wastebasket which sounded like the dropping of an anchor, so they used that too. No, I never got a royalty.

Let's see what else can I remember about the studio? Well, there are one or two other things but its best we move on. I can see at this rate I'll never have a chance to get through half of this stuff. I suppose I could always make a sequel. You know, Part Two.

Okay, what's next?

Item Four—Small boxes of reel recordings sent in by a fan

These are pretty interesting, The Beatles got so much fan mail it was ridiculous. Very early on Brian Epstein had set up an official fan club and they had their own monthly magazine. It had a big circulation, I'm not sure exactly how big, but it loaded us down with a lot of mail, and not just mail, but with toys, and cookies, and dolls, gifts of all shapes and sizes, and of course cards and letters and drawings and all manner of craziness. But the best of all were these reel recordings they used to send in. Really they were nothing other than girls gushing about their love and crushes on The Beatles. Sometimes they sing them their songs or worse, write an sing their own. It was really fun listening to them. John's limo, which I mostly drove, had all this audio equipment installed in the back console. And with really big speakers. The Beatles were really into sound recordings themselves, obviously, and they rarely went out without their own recorders in case they would think of an idea for a song of something. Except Ringo of course. He usually carried around cameras because he was a photography buff.

Anyway, these tapes are in my possession because John gave them to me that last afternoon when we were sorting through the car. I haven't heard them in years because I don't have a tape player that plays this old-fashioned tape size. But I know what's on them, mostly just a lot of nonsense and fun and games and foolish banter and that sort of thing. The Beatles really were an irreverent lot and they never stopped teasing each other or me or Neil or Mal. And they never stopped teasing other motorists or pedestrians as we sped by. My point is that they saved a fortune in recoding media by simply recording over these fan tapes. We had hundreds of them. John and Paul both kept theirs in shelves in their home studios. I'm not sure where George kept his. I wonder where they all are now? In some library archive I hope. I'll have to find out and donate these as well.

What's next? Let's see. I hope I'm not boring you as I putter about here.

Item Five - A photograph of The Beatles and their wives/girlfriends

Okay, let me fill you in on their personal lives a little bit. Here's a photo of John and Cynthia Lennon, his first wife and the mother of Julian Lennon. They got married back in 1962 or 1963 but in any event, by the time they became major pop stars, they were already married. They had met each other at Liverpool Art College in the late 50's and were an item for several years. Cynthia and a girlfriend even went to visit the boys in Hamburg in 1962. My point about telling you all this is that once they made it big, Brian thought it would be a catastrophe if word leaked out that one of The Beatles was married. And that she was expecting. So, for about the first year of their success Cynthia had to lie low and on many occasions, when cornered by the press or by fans, had to deny being married to John. And when that got old, she denied even being herself. She was just being loyal but I have no doubt that time she found it a little bit disconcerting. But there wasn't much she could do about it. John was traveling around non-stop and based in London. She was in Liverpool either living with John's aunt Mimi or in a small flat with her own mother. She once told me she never asked John for a penny and that he never offered her one. That's how fast everything happened. And everyone was unprepared.

Well, by the end of 1964 she was allowed to surface. And for the most part they did their best to lead a quiet home life together, along with their young son. I visited them at home often, sometimes every day for weeks on end. As a general rule Cynthia was pretty normal, pretty well-grounded. Of course you'd have to be to put up with somebody as ornery as John Lennon. They had a nice big house in what John called "the stockbroker's belt" of south London. It took almost a year to renovate it and for the longest time they lived in servant's quarters in the rear of the home. John and I used to take tea in the garden or the garage just to get away from all the sound of the workmen.

Ringo was the second to marry, I remember it well because I was with him the several days before the wedding, and I drove him and his bride to and from her register's office. Her name was Maureen Cox and she was also from Liverpool. He had met her somewhere, I can't recall but she was working at a hair salon and she just got to him somehow. Ringo said it was love at first sight but when you looked at her, being just seventeen, I suppose any man might have wanted her. She was a beauty. And to top it off, she was actually quite charming and had a nice personality, certainly, just like Cynthia Lennon, Maureen Starkey kept Ringo grounded, and let me tell you, that was not an easy thing to do. They got married in early 1965 in London. They went on a brief honeymoon to East Sussex where they stayed at the country home of The Beatles solicitor David Jacobs. The press hounded us along the way and wouldn't leave until the young couple made a few innocent comments at a make shirt press conference. I spent the rest of the evening partying with the Cox family at a London restaurant. It was the first time I felt like an insider, a friend, and not just as a chauffeur and bodyguard. That's one positive thing I can say about The Beatles, they never made me feel like a servant. I was always their friend and assistant. Just like Neil and Mal. They were very generous to my wife and I and never forgot our birthdays or our anniversary and the like. You'd think they'd have too much on their minds to bother, but no. They remembered us.

Paul had a girlfriend named Jane Asher and she was from London. She was an aspiring actress, and her mother and father were a lovely couple, he a psychiatrist and she a fashionable 1960's housewife, who incidentally, was formerly a music teacher. It turns out she once gave oboe lessons to The Beatles' producer George Martin. Jane had a younger brother and sister as I recall. Her brother Peter became a pop star in his own right with a duo called Peter and Gordon. Several years later he went to work for Apple as the head of its in-house talent agency.

Paul and Jane were a hot item around town and they were always being barraged by the press as to when they planned to marry. They got engaged in 1966 but never married. Paul says she would never let him set a date. In reality, she had her own career and was always doubtful she could pursue it and maintain a relationship with a real-life Beatle. God knows it was a challenge for them both just to be together. That's why they used to hang out in clubs like the Ad Lib or Scotch at St. James'. They were private clubs where The Beatles and their women could hang out and not be disturbed by fans or journalists or photographers. I used to drive them and indeed all the boys and their dates to the clubs all the time, sometimes three and four nights a week. And often after long recording sessions. They used to love to go out and sometimes they stayed out all night, and we'd go home with the milkman, as they used to say.

Paul was the only one of The Beatles that didn't have his own home in London during the early days so Mrs. Asher invited him to move in with them. And he did so for nearly two years. They had a big old house and he lived in a suite of rooms on the top floor. I remember going over to their house and picking Paul up on many occasions. Mrs. Asher would always invite me in for breakfast. She made the best eggs in the world, Paul and I shared many mornings and afternoons at the Asher dining table. He always said that when he wrote the song Yesterday he first called it Scrambled Eggs. No doubt in tribute to Mrs. Asher's delicious breakfasts.

George was of course the youngest and shyest of The Beatles but he soon blossomed right along the rest of them. He met the love of his life, a beautiful woman named Pattie Boyd, while filming on the set of "A Hard Day's Night." She was a young fashion model and somehow she got the call to work in the film as an extra. He took an instant liking to her and tried to court her but she was rather cool, later explaining to him when he finally got her alone that she was already engaged. But George, feeling the hubris that only a twenty-two-year-old Beatle/millionaire can feel, pursued her until she agreed to go out with him. She was as sweet, innocent and gorgeous as they came. The very essence of swinging London; mini skirt and all. After a couple of dates separated by his grueling schedule, he took her out to tour a house he was thinking of buying in Esher, south of London near John's place. When she saw the place modern kind of place that was not very big but was well protected and had a nice pool and garden, she must have said yes when he asked her to help him decorate it so they could live there together, and that's just what they did. They got married in January 1966. Again, I dove them to the civil registers office and was a witness to the ceremony. Paul and Brian Epstein shared the role of best man. And of course, the press was everywhere. We tried to keep it a secret but somehow word leaked out. It usually did.

I should mention for a minute a little bit about the security we tried to maintain for the boys, because security was really the basis of my job. You can't very well trust a bloody chauffer if you don't think you're going to be safe with him. I always got my instructions directly from Brian or his secretary or his assistant Alistair. This was both before and after I was made a NEMS employee and thus an official part of The Beatles entourage, which mind you was always just a handful of people, not like the pop stars of today travel around with. Our security was basically non-existent except for what I could do to look after them, along with Neil and Mal, of course. Our idea of security was principally trying to keep things secret, meaning out of the press. That's what we worried about most. We relied upon the Metropolitan police in London and the local constabularies just about everywhere else. And for the most part they were very good to us. Let's put it this way, with all the tearing around I did with one of more of them in the car, we came across an awful lot of policeman but nary a one gave me a traffic citation or even a cross word or glance. In all of my travels with The Beatles and in the hundreds and hundreds of times I took them around somewhere, I was the only bodyguard they ever had.

Another funny thing they used to do, and this was purely Paul's idea, was run around in disguises. I think he must have gotten the idea from his girlfriend Jane being an actress and seeing her in her dressing room and such. He collected all kinds of moustaches and wigs and glasses and such that we kept in the car just in case they were needed.

I remember one day in particular when Paul called me up and asked me to take him antiquing. We were served our customary breakfast by Mrs. Asher and then he excused himself from the table. The next thing I know there he is in a long beard, glasses and an overcoat saying, "Okay Alfie, I'm ready. Let's go." And it worked too, until we had lunch together that afternoon, just the two of us, in a pub on Portobello Road in central London. We were busted by a Welsh waitress. She was onto us and she started whispering to her co-workers in the pub. I could see what was about to happen so we drank up our beers, left a fiver on the table and got the hell out of there before Paul could be set upon by the masses present there. It would have happened no doubt. That's the way it was when you were with a Beatle. Always subject to attack by wildly enthusiastic fans. Or by the ever present photographers or autograph hounds and just about everyone else. It was utterly chaotic. But frankly we all got a high from it and rarely felt a sense of real danger. That was to come later.

Let's move on, shall we?

Item Six—A woman's underwear, still with price tag attached

What more can you say about these? Women were always giving The Beatles their panties. A symbolic gesture no doubt. This particular pair of panties was tied one day in I think Sheffield to the antenna of the Austin Princess, which is the car I most frequently drove the boys around in. That was on our UK tour in November 1964. I kept it because it has a note written write on to the material. It reads: "Dearest Paul If you ring me I'll show you where these belong, signed Melinda G. with her phone number" Of course I didn't give this to him. I'd be passed notes and gifts all the time for the boys. It's impossible to refuse to accept them, coming usually as they did, from ecstatic young girls. Paul had enough trouble with women trying to get him in the sack. I figure he didn't need my help. It's still new, here's the sales tag. All those years ago.

Item Seven—A copy of Brian Epstein's autobiography, *A Cellarful of Noise*

Here's a nice piece of memorabilia, an autographed copy of Brian Epstein's autobiography *A Cellarful of Noise*, which of course relates to The Cavern Club, where he first chanced upon The Beatles at the end of 1961. This is a good time to talk a little about Brian because nobody today really remembers anything about him, except that he was The Beatles' manager and died young. Those who know a little more about him maybe know that he was Jewish and a closeted homosexual.

I never knew Brian very well myself but I had the opportunity to speak with him and drive him around on a number of occasions. Even though he was obviously very close to The Beatles, he wasn't actually with them all that often, except when they went on foreign tours. For the most part, he communicated with them by phone and by a flurry of very un-memorable memos about everything under the sun. I only remember that he was a true gentleman and a very shy fellow who had tremendous responsibilities and generally carried them out very well. But they liked him very much and I think for the most part, respected everything he was doing for them. And believe me, it required lots of hard work and long days and nights. Thank God he had a good core staff of people that helped him out at NEMS.

Brian was also from Liverpool and in 1961 he was working for his father in the family's department store called Epstein's. He had gotten into music back when the new craze was called skiffle. He, like The Beatles themselves was totally impressed by early American rock n rollers like Elvis of course, and Bill Haley and Buddy Holly and Big Bill Brunzy and Roy Orbison and Carl Perkins and Eddie Cochran and the like. Seeing that it was the next big thing, he convinced his mother and father to let him open up a music store in the basement of their store, and after a short time it became very successful.

Now what is not well-known by anybody actually, is that Brian had a friend named Joe Flannery who was managing his younger brother's band called Lee Curtis and the All-Stars. They were one of the many bands that were laying down the Mersey Beat at the same time as The Beatles. Anyway, this gives Brian the idea that he too would like to manage a band and that's how he found The Beatles; at the Cavern Club playing the lunch time set. It was said that he fell in love with John, and that's what really motivated him. God only knows, but the fact is he offered to manage them, and they agreed. This was the beginning of 1962. Everything they achieved until the day of his death in August 1967, they achieved together.

Speaking of Joe Flannery and Lee Curtis, here's a little story not many people know. It concerns the origin of The Beatles' mop-top haircuts, which were as revolutionary as their music when they burst onto the scene in 1963. Joe's mother was a jitterbug dancer in the 20's and there was a photograph of her in her costume in their front room. Her hair was cut in bangs over her forehead. Brian saw that photo and it must have registered in his mind. Once he started managing the boys, he took them out of leathers and jeans and put them into those famous tailored suits. And with the suits came the look and the do.

Epstein's company NEMS stood for North End Music Store. I could tell you a lot more about Brian and his associates and his dealing with the boys, but that's a story in and of itself. It turns out that he, like the boys at the time, was badly addicted to both amphetamines and barbiturates; acid and downers of all shapes and sizes and colors. And on top of that he was taking both pre-scribed and black market medications. Plus, he liked to drink scotch and gin. One night, feeling depressed, he took a few too many and overdosed. He would be the first of a whole slew of rock n roll personalities who would go the same way. To me he was always a gentleman. Brian Epstein, rest in peace.

Moving on. Are you still with me folks?

Item Eight—August 1964 copy of Life magazine with The Beatles on the cover

What more can you say about this? August 1964 Life magazine, this was during The Beatles' first tour of America and Canada. They were heralded as the vanguard of the British invasion. More welcome than the redcoats I imagine.

Item Nine—Photo of Beatles with their MBE awards

Here is a nice photograph of the boys on a very special day. It was October 26, 1965, the day they received their MBE awards from Queen Elizabeth. What a bunch of controversy that created. Of course, they were made members of the British empire largely because of their charity concerts and in recognition of the success they achieved for British exports, namely their records. But an awful lot of people felt that pop stars where not on the same level as war heroes and philanthropists and shouldn't be recognized by the queen as such. I figure they felt it marginalized their own orders. Consequently, many threatened to send theirs back, and some actually did. It was the first real controversy The Beatles found themselves embroiled in. For the most part they just laughed it off. It wouldn't be so easy with future controversies, let me tell you.

What's next, what's next? Oh yes.

Item Ten—A copy of the LP *Help!*

When I first got close to The Beatles, I mean when I became their permanent driver, they were beginning the recording sessions of songs for their next film, which was supposed to be called "Eight Arms to Hold You" but ended up becoming *Help!* Brian had made a three picture deal with an American producer and this was the second film of that deal. *A Hard Day's Night* had been a sensation and they wanted to rush out another while the boys were still hot. I think even then it was pretty much thought that they wouldn't last so they were pushing The Beatles to make the next one quickly. They had been working on the songs but the problem is they didn't have a script. When that was finally sorted out we went right from the studio to filming. Because The Beatles' accountants advised them that they would pay a lot less taxes if they incorporated the film in The Bahamas, they said they ought to film some of it there too. I drove them all to the airport but didn't go with them.

They came back after about ten days and had just a day or two turnaround, during which they each kept me busy as ever running them around here and there and getting this and that for them. Then I drove them back to Heathrow for a two week trip to Austria where the skiing scenes were filmed, in the Alps. Then they got back and over the period of the next month or so they were kept busy almost every day either filming, recording, clubbing or partying… sometimes all in one day. It was crazy. Everywhere they went was pure pandemonium. The reason I remember this all so vividly is for two reasons really. First is that all the time during the endless days of filming on location and in the Twickenham movie studio, I was reduced to being The Beatles' manservant. Here I am serving them tea on a very windy and chilly morning on Salisbury Plain. We had half a platoon of British soldiers to help us. Their MPs kept the press and fans at bay. Day after day week after week that's all I did was wait upon The Beatles. "Alf will you please do this or go and get that or help with this or deliver that." Or whatever. I can't say I minded at all, that was my job and I was having a ball. I knew where I was and I knew how lucky I was to be there. No complaints here. Never were, except of course for the lack of sleep.

The other thing I remember about the *Help!* period is being introduced to cannabis. Marijuana. Pot, as they called it. I was actually very naïve back then. One day on the way to the studio, it may have been the first day, I'm not sure, I smell something burning in the in the back of the car. I asked them what was on fire and they're just laughing and joking. John says something like, "Just keep your eye on the road mate." Then Ringo said, "Don't worry about us Alf we've got it all under control." Then Paul said something I didn't understand and they all started howling. I figured if they were in such I good mood who am I to try and spoil it.

A day or two later when we were at the studio or somewhere, Neil asks me to drive him to his flat, which was near Ringo's place. So I did and he invites me in. So I followed him and he grabs a beer and offers me one and sits on his couch all relaxed like. Now I was rather surprised because he told me we were just going to fetch something he forgot. Next thing I know he pulls out this paper bag from beneath the couch, takes another bag out of it and then opens it and spreads it out on the table in front of him. Then he asked me for a pack of cigarette papers, which I had and I gave him.

"This," he says, "is pot. Do you know what that is Alf?" "Yeah of course I know," I says. And I was being truthful because I knew what it was; I had just never seen any before or ever came across it. "I'm going to roll a few joints for the boys. Do you mind?"

"Of course not, "I replied. What the hell was I supposed to say? It was none of my business really. But after that their behavior towards me changed, I was suddenly "in." I went from being an employee to being one of the team. It was really that simple. George later told me he was relieved that I knew. They didn't like the idea of hiding it from me. They had to be secretive enough I figured and didn't like having to keep it on the hush-hush around me. Fine by me. They were The Beatles. Who was I to interfere with their fun or their lifestyles? I thought it was fine. Little did I know that I would soon become, in addition to chauffer and bodyguard, their chief pot custodian. I could tell you a hundred stories about all the crazy things I had to do to hide the pot when we went from country to country on tour, but again, that's a whole story in itself.

I will tell you this, I later learned from Neil that they were turned on to pot by none other than Bob Dylan when they met him in NYC the previous September. They really dug the shit. Pretty much the entire time they filmed "Help!" The Beatles were high. That's pretty much the way they stayed for a long time afterward.

Okay, let's move on.

Item Eleven—A Japanese lacquer box, in which is held an ashtray

These bring back memories that's for sure. They arrived in the mail a few months after I left The Beatles employ. They were purchased by John I think, when we were in Japan in the beginning of July 1966. That was the craziest time of all, the world tour of 1966. It was also the scariest. Let me give you a little context. Up until that point The Beatles could do no wrong. But 1966 was nothing but one headache after the other, that's why I eventually called it quits. It was just too damn chaotic.

Thankfully the year opened like the year before ended, with lots of good news and high notes. George got married and then celebrated his 24th birthday. They had songs topping the charts all over the world. They all took nice vacations in exotic places. The BBC showed a documentary film on television all about The Beatles' Shea Stadium concert the previous summer. I was there and with them the entire time but I had no idea of all that went on. It was even crazier than we all knew. Then   "Yesterday" hits the charts and it's a smash. And I remember taking all the boys and their girls to the premiere of Jane Asher's new film "Alfie," which I got to see with them and which was great. They teased me about my name the whole night and kept singing to me "What's it all about, Alfie?" If you've never seen that film, I highly recommend you do. It gives a good idea of what the scene was like in the Swinging

'60's London. As usual we probably went clubbing afterward for another grand night out. It may have been Dolly's or it could have been The Flamingo, it was all the same. The Beatles went out often and partied hardy. They were often joined by many friends, lots of pop stars from the UK and America and the like. They far preferred their own kind to the silly hangers-on that always tried to get close to them. I'm talking about the DJ's, the city elite, rich men's sons and daughters and such. During these binges I met the like of Mick Jagger and some of the Stones, members of The Dave Clark Five, The Beach Boys, The Bryds, the Ronnettes and all kinds of Motown singers (whose music The Beatles really admired), oh there were so many others, don't get me started. It's not my intention to drop names, please forgive me if it sounds like that. I just want you to appreciate the draw these boys had. Everyone wanted to meet them and they were always eager and curious to meet new people too. The Beatles loved talent and respected it. I think this is something they learned from Brian Epstein. Remember, Brian had lots of other acts under management and The Beatles were frequently called upon to help them out as well. They never refused.

So what was I talking about? Right, 1966. Let's see. In the Spring they went into the studio to record the songs that made up the LPs *Revolver* and *Rubber Soul*. That was a good time, very productive. This was the first time they started to do really creative things in the studio, like playing with tape speeds, running thru things backward, using studio musicians to create new sounds, and all sorts of other things. Don't get me started.

A list of the songs from those two LPs appears on the screen: here, just look at them. The titles speak for themselves. I can tell you a story about the recording of every one of them, but we just don't have the time. Sorry. There are lots of accounts in all those Beatles books about these days but I was there. I know how it all went down. It was fucking fantastic.

I can also remember taking the boys to see some concerts they wanted to attend. They saw and met afterwards, Stevie Wonder, Bob Dylan, Roy Orbison, Johnnie Mathis, Judy Garland, Joan Baez, and a lot of others. It was always a joy to be with them when they were meeting fellow celebrities.

The year before, during the 1965 tour of America, we met lots and lots of Hollywood stars at a party thrown for The Beatles at the LA home of a Capitol Records executive. We met Groucho Marx, Jack Benny, Gene Berry, Tony Bennett, Dean Martin, Rock Hudson, Gregory Peck, Kirk Douglas, and so many others I can't even remember. I remember meeting Mr. and Mrs. Jimmy Stewart, who I had met some years before in London on a driving assignment. They remembered me and even invited me to go back to their house for dinner. But I had to decline, Brian wouldn't let me attend. Can't blame him really, I was on their time not my own. But do you think James Stewart would have invited me to his home for dinner if I hadn't been working for The Beatles? Not a chance. They were that infectious. No doubt he would have wanted me to bring autographed photos and records for his grand kids. Hey, who could blame him? They were huge.

Anyway, that was the same time we also met Elvis Presley, which for me and the boys was a stand-out occasion. I don't need to go into the details but we were invited to his home in the hills above Hollywood somewhere. I think it was just the eight of us, the four boys, me, Neil, Mal and Brian. Maybe our press guy Tony Barrow was with us, I can't remember. Anyway, here we were, about to meet the king. The Beatles were all very excited because they loved his music and always considered him an icon … even though he hadn't had a hit in a few years…but his movies were very popular. And when we arrived, there was Elvis greeting each of us at the door. I was the last one in and I remember Elvis shaking my hand and patting by back, "Welcome to my home, sir," he said to me. I'll never forget it. Elvis called me sir. Amazing. Well we had a hell of a good time. I remember one thing in particular. As the evening wore on, Ringo and I were sitting by the pool table just watching everyone across the large room. I'm guessing there were about twenty-five people or so there, including Elvis' wife and daughter, Col. Tom Parker his manager, friends of Elvis who we later learned were called the Memphis Mafia, and mostly Elvis' people.

As I was watching them, I turned and said to Ringo, "You know Ritchie, there are about ten of them taking care of Elvis and he's only one. But there are only three of us taking care of the four of you." Ringo looked at me, he was pretty drunk at the time, and said, nonchalantly, "What are you getting at Alf, do you want a rise?" We just laughed. It was great.

They sent us away with lots of little gifts. It was an evening I'll always remember. The following night some of Elvis' men took me and Mal out around town in chauffeured limos. We had a beautiful dinner and visited a few clubs. We stayed out very late. Brian was quite perturbed at us the following day. Can't say I blame him now, looking back on it. But who could refuse an invitation like that? When were we going to spend another night with Elvis for all we knew?

I remember the day The Beatles got stoned with Peter Fonda in a big hot tub at the house they were renting in Benedict Canyon. I remember one day when two girls jumped out of a helicopter and into the pool at the house. Almost killed themselves trying to see

The Beatles. I escorted them right out of there. I remember when they played the Hollywood Bowl. Oh so many memories of that first trip to California.

Getting back to '66, then came the controversy over the butcher baby photographs that were used as artwork for the cover of the new single Paperback Writer. I thought they were in really bad taste, but I kept it to myself, or I may have mentioned it to Mal or something. But it just wasn't my place to say anything critically about their artistic decisions. I kept clear of the whole scene because I didn't want my suit to get splattered with cow blood. But I wrote my reservations in my diary just so I could always say I told you so, Anyway, they were in poor taste to say the least but in England nobody raised to much of a fuss about them, which looking back, I find hard to believe. But when Capitol Records in the US used the photo as the cover shot for The Beatles new LP in America, one they called *Yesterday and Today*. It created a furor and Capitol had a nightmare trying to recall them all and it cost them a fortune. They blamed Brian Epstein but if you ask me it was their own damn fault. Anyway, it cast a pall over their work because everyone sort-of self-righteously said afterward, "What in the hell were they thinking?" It was a very embarrassing event, to say the least.

Let's move on. Directly after those sessions finished, we set off for the first part of our world tour. Mind you, it wasn't a world tour like you have today. First, we went to West Germany and played a few concerts there, including a triumphal return to Hamburg, where The Beatles played so many months in 1961 and 1962. They hooked up with lots of old friends, it was great. They were loving it. I remember thinking to myself that last night in Hamburg when we were all out at some rathskeller toasting it up, how odd it was that the people of Hamburg, a major German port city only twenty years before were bombing the hell out of the people of Liverpool, another great port city. And they were giving it right back. And here we all were together, Germans and Brits drinking and laughing together. I can't help but feel it was the power of The Beatles' music that done it.

Next it was off to Japan. We left Hamburg in a big to-do because it was the inaugural flight of this particular route to Tokyo. They gave us nice kimonos and welcomed us beautifully. But a few hours later we were told that due to a storm or something we would have to be diverted to Anchorage, Alaska. Which we were, and we spent the night in a motel there with very few people knowing what The Beatles were about. It was all kept hush-hush even to the other passengers. The Beatles tour party had the entire first-class section reserved. I would guess there were ten or twelve of us in total. Epstein and a few of his people, the four boys, Neil, Mal and I. That was it. Well believe it or not, we found a bar and partied in it for a bit and then we all fell asleep until the next afternoon, when they told us to get ready because they plane was leaving in two hours. It was my job to get them all up. Let me tell you, that weren't easy. But we finally made it to Tokyo and the first thing we noticed is all the security and so few fan welcomers. Now remember, The Beatles are met at every airport by thousands of screaming fans. I mean, that's just understood. But it wasn't like that in Tokyo that day. There were about a hundred fans all hemmed into one area in the terminal but there was what seemed like five hundred police and soldiers. It was a rude awakening.

Well, it turns out what had happened is that a whole hullabaloo got started about where The Beatles were scheduled to perform, a modern big auditorium called The Budokan. The problem is, this big new auditorium had been dedicated as a kind of martial arts sanctum and it was used for ceremonies of some kind. Hordes of Japanese fanatics deplored it being used by pop stars playing western music. They thought it would defile the hall. Of course, we had nothing to do with it. But as a consequence, The Beatles were getting death threats and there were real concerns that a riot might erupt in the streets. We were advised of this situation once we got to our hotel, the Tokyo Hilton. It was terrible and Brian tried to smooth things over by holding a press conference but the idea was scrapped because the authorities were afraid he might say something to make matters worse. I remember the Japanese promoters of the show, were under 24-hour guard. We felt horrible for them when we learned this.

Anyway, it was all quite disconcerting, to say the least. We did our two shows and they went off pretty well. It's just that the fans didn't scream nearly as loudly and the hall was half filled with police up and down the aisles. They were afraid somebody might stand up and shoot The Beatles. I asked a police captain in charge of our security if the audience would be searched at the doors. He said this was against Japanese custom. They didn't have metal detectors in those days. Thus, all the police in the venue.

The bizarre aspect to this situation was that we were virtual prisoners in our hotel suites, which were on our own floor right at the top, very well guarded. I remember the uniformed officers everywhere. We couldn't speak to them of course because we couldn't. But because The Beatles couldn't see Tokyo, Tokyo was brought to them. All day long we would get visitors of all kinds to show us goods like cameras and jewelry and we got lots of gifts, like this lacquer box and ashtray, for example. The promoters went out and rounded up about a dozen geisha girls. Believe it or not we didn't know what to do with them they were so damn proper, and the boys were so damn irreverent. It was hilarious is what it was. They were treated like royalty, really. We were sad to leave in a way because the Japanese were so thoughtful to us, to our every need. But we were off to The Philippines, where it really got ugly.

Now I won't go into this in too much detail because again, it is a very long story. We were looking forward to these shows because The Beatles were really big in The Philippines and they were among the most loyal fans they had. Everything was great at the beginning. Like usual we were met by local dignitaries and the promoters with big limos to take us to our hotel. Lots of screaming fans were there to greet the boys, again, as usual. But instead of going to our hotel we were taken out to a pier in Manila Harbor, escorted to a waiting ship and motored out to a yacht that was anchored in the bay. This was supposed to be where we were to stay. But Brian and the boys wanted nothing of it. It seemed like a good idea to me, coming as we did from Tokyo were we were so confined. Then I realized that all our luggage was still on the shore in a van, where I made sure it was placed before we were sped off from the airport. Suddenly in a panic I whispered to Neil that the pot was in a travel case marked "technical gear." His eyes opened wide and he immediately told Paul or John or someone and that sealed it. We returned straight back to the pier collected our things and headed to our hotel, as was previously arranged. Everything went pretty much according to plan from then out. The Beatles played two shows at a huge stadium. As usual it was pandemonium, but things went off well. I witnessed a lot of police brutality against ecstatic fans but it was but my place to interfere. There were so few of us and so many of them. There was nothing we could do.

Then all hell broke loose, We're back at the hotel after the first show and a big controversy erupts. It seems the first lady of the land, one Imelda Marcos, had invited The Beatles to a luncheon reception in the garden of the presidential palace, and they stood her up. There were three hundred children there and she cried openly during the event because they didn't arrive. Suddenly all these military people come to our hotel rooms and summon Brian to ask him when The Beatles are planning to go to the presidential palace. He didn't know what they were talking about. The boys were knackered and weren't going anywhere. What the general who was in charge apparently wanted was for The Beatles to go over to the palace and apologize. Well that just wasn't going to happen. It turns out an invitation had been sent to one of Brian's people in Japan but nothing was done about it. It was a public relations catastrophe. While Brian was negotiating with the president's officials, I was sent back and forth between them and the boys' rooms to deliver messages. Nothing doing, they didn't want to go. Even then they knew Marcos was a dictator and wanted nothing to do with him. Then the British ambassador called. I was asked to speak with him but what in the world am I supposed to say. "Who the hell am I?" I thought. I could say something and get us all in even bigger trouble. Finally, after about another hour or so of real tension, Brian offered to go on national television and offer an explanation that there had been a misunderstanding about the event and there was no intention to slight the first lady or the Filipino people. In addition, he was to offer a very generous donation to Mrs. Marco's children's charity.

But all of a sudden everything changed. We noticed all our security had been withdrawn. We made a mad dash for the airport which was pure hell. A gang of thugs who we mistook for fans at first, kicked and jeered us as we ran through the terminal. I was personally assaulted and knocked to the ground carrying all these ivory gifts that Brian had purchased. My only thought was that some may have gotten broke. There is a photo of me getting helped back up but little did everyone know that it was by the same guys who punched me down. It was pure mayhem. I can't even believe we made it aboard, but not before getting searched and demeaned by customs police. It was ugly. Then once we were all on board, some police came on the plane and escorted Brian and Mal Evans off the plane. Now mind you, we still hadn't had our passports returned and we're think something is definitely on. My first thought was they found the pot in the instrument case, and I figured we might not see them again. Mal was nearly in tears as he was led off the plane. Minutes seemed like hours. Finally, after Brian begged the KLM pilot not to leave them stranded, and the pilot intervened, were they allowed back on. It turns out they had to post a bond and sign some papers. We left the Philippines without getting paid and by the skin of our teeth. When we were finally airborne, tempers flared from everybody in our party. The Beatles were really angry with Brian, who was really angry at Vic Lewis, who was really angry at Mal, for what I don't know. It took an hour in the air before things cooled down. But after that things were never really the same. It was that harrowing.

Of course it all hit the papers but the true story was never really disclosed. "Beatles Roughed Up in Manila" was what the headlines screamed. That sort of thing. It was arranged that they'd fly to New Delhi directly from Manila, for a few days of rest. George had really been getting into Indian music and John I think was quite keen on it too. Everyone I think knows that the sitar first appeared on John's song Norwegian Wood. And then on some other songs by George. Anyway, due to the incident in Manila, what was supposed to be a quiet holiday turned into a bit of a mess. We just weren't free to move about. We had to sneak out everywhere in disguises. It was just the four of them, Neil and I. Great memories. Ringo has all the photographs, he snapped them all the time. Of course, The Beatles went back to India in 1967 when they got involved with the mystic Maharishi Yogi and his whole Transcendental Meditation movement. But I wasn't around for that. I heard it was a fiasco too. The Maharishi tried to use them and when they got onto that, they bailed on him. It was a big mess too. It was pretty clear to everybody involved that being a Beatle was not always fun or easy.

Well, we were happy to be back in London. That's all I can say. But just as we were getting our balance back, things even got uglier. This whole "Beatles thing is more popular than the Jesus thing" hit the papers. In America it was a firestorm of controversy. Here, take a look at this cartoon that John gave me that final day.

Item Twelve—Newspaper comic illustration

It pretty much sums it up. The Beatles were under fire like never before and the really sad thing about it is that there was nothing to it. It was all blown out of proportion by a bunch of holier-than-thou fools from America. In an interview that John gave to a close friend, a London journalist named Maureen Cleave, he got all philosophical. It was supposed to be an in-depth piece. The point is that this interview was conducted months earlier and was published in London with nary a fuss. But parts of it were picked up by a US magazine in late July and the part where John said The Beatles were more popular than Jesus Christ was picked up on, completely out of context, and taken to be sacrilegious. Within days there were protests in cities in America, burning of their LPs and calls to ban their music from the radio, which a whole bunch of Bible-belt radios stations in fact did do.

I just happened to be in the NEMS office when it all broke loose. It was a miasma of disbelief. Everyone was trying to get ahold of Brian but he was sick at the time with glandular fever and somewhere in Wales recuperating. Pretty soon there was talk of canceling the whole tour. Alistair Taylor told me this would have resulted in a financial catastrophe for them. And to make matters worse, they had already got a big advance on the US record sales, and wholesalers and distributors where pulling them off the market.

Word finally got through to Brian and was whisked out of Wales directly to NYC at the instance of Capital Records. He gave a press conference in which he tried to explain that John meant nothing of the sort, but John refused to let him apologize. That was something that was discussed over the phone. John was adamant about that. He said he said what he said and he was not ashamed of it. Brian was therefore forced to simply try and explain it away. It probably helped but it didn't go away. But he did hold together the tour promising personally to cover the losses the US promoters might sustain. Of course it was; the tour was an advance sell-out everywhere. If there were cancellations, it would have busted us completely. It was that precarious.

Five days later The Beatles, with me along for the ride, arrived in Chicago for the first stop on the tour. They first thing we did once we got to the hotel was a big press conference to try and quiet things down. And the press that evening was menacing as hell. They just kept driving at John until after explaining himself three or four times finally said he was sorry for saying whatever it was he said that people found so offensive. That he didn't mean anything antic Christian by it. It wasn't easy for him, I know. I was watching him the whole time and my heart really went out to him. Poor old John, he didn't deserve it. And the rest of The Beatles were pretty upset by the whole thing too. They rallied around him like true and honest friends. It was hoped that would be the last of it. But sadly, it wasn't. All of a sudden, their getting death threats again and security is beefed up in every city we go. It was obvious no police chief or mayor wanted an incident with The Beatles on their clocks. That's when I started sitting on stage right behind the boys, to protect them in case any irate fans tried to charge them. I remember when we got to Memphis there was a bomb scare and John only half-jokingly asked me to crawl beneath the stage to see if I could find one. It was all pretty hellish.

On that tour we played about twenty cities and thankfully, despite all the headaches and constant problems, we made every show. We visited Minneapolis, Detroit, Cincinnati, (where The Beatles almost got electrocuted because nobody thought to cover the stadium stage in the event of rain…which it of course did), Washington DC, Toronto, Montreal, Boston, St. Louis, Houston, Atlanta, Shea Stadium again in NYC; then we went out to play Dodger Stadium in LA, the Seattle and finally to Candlestick Park in San Francisco. By pre-arrangement it was decided that this was going to be the final Beatles concert. The boys had definitely had enough.

It was a whale of a show too. The boys really enjoyed themselves. Here's a good photo of yours truly at that show grabbing another fan and ushering her off stage to the police. It was pandemonium, as usual. Mal, Neil and I each played stage guard duty. It was both frightening and exhilarating. And while we're trying to protect them from crazies, The Beatles were having a ball on stage. Till my last day on earth I'll never cease to remember the looks on those fans faces. Sheer hysteria. It utterly amazed me. And I remember how happy the boys were when they were playing together. It was fantastic.

When the show was over (The Beatles never played encores because it was just too difficult to stage manage them) we were back in the dressing rooms, which were really huge I remember and the press was jostling to get in. When we finally shooed them all away, the boys Mal, Neil and I were there all exhausted and sweaty, having a beer and trying to come back down to earth. The adrenaline that runs through your system under those conditions just can't be explained. It's wild. A super-high. But you need to come down after all that rushing and screaming and poking and such. So, there we are just trying to calm down a bit and John finally says, "Well that's it for me lads, the final Beatles show." George raised his hands in the air, waving his towel around and said, "Hooray, I'm no longer a Beatle." There was what seemed like a long awkward pause and then I said, "Okay then, that's it for me. I think I'll pack it in too." Nobody said a word. I really think everyone felt the same way.

There are only a few more things I want to talk about. After I left their employ in November 1966, I stayed up on their career and remained friends with Alistair Taylor, probably their most loyal management company employee. He and a few others did their best to hold the business together after Brian's death, but it was not easy. The whole business side of The Beatles' story is something I really don't know that much about because it was so damn complicated. In the end, it was business and taxes that broke them apart.

It was 1967, the Summer Love, and LSD, brought *Sergeant Pepper* and *Magical Mystery Tour*, the whole concept of Apple Records and of course the Apple Boutique. 1968 brought the *Yellow Submarine* movie, *The White Album*, and Yoko Ono to live as one with John, as they described it. From then on, because of this "artistic union," The Beatles were five and no longer four. Despite the stress of their relationship and the challenges that lawsuits and business entanglements brought them, they still managed to make some great music. Nineteen hundred and sixty-nine opened with the simultaneous recording and filming of *Let It Be*, which turned into a big mess in itself, so much so that the entire project was shelved. That famous concert they gave on the roof of their Apple headquarters was the last spurt of that project since the whole project was supposed to conclude with a live performance. So, they started all over again and came up with their most critically acclaimed album, Abbey Road, which was their swan song. And it was their very biggest selling album by far. An absolute masterpiece it is.

John married Yoko and a week later Paul married Linda Eastman. They started going their separate ways and working on solo projects. John and Yoko got politically active, Paul secluded himself in at his farm in Scotland, George got deeply into Buddhism, and Ringo when he wasn't horsing around with film roles and playing billiards, his passion, played very much the family man with his wife Maureen and their two sons.

Here's one last item of interest.

Item Thirteen - Book about Manson family murders.

Oh yes, 1969 was also the year a lunatic named Charles Manson claimed that some of the song lyrics from *The White Album* were encrypted messages to commit murder and try to trigger a race riot across America. He called it Helter Skelter, after the song. It was an ugly business to have your art used for such purposes and John and Paul especially were completely revolted by it all. And those gruesome murders pretty much served as a kind of end cap on the '60's. But have you ever thought of what the '60's would be like without The Beatles? They just wouldn't be the sixties. Their influence was extraordinary, both musically and culturally. They fashioned a look, a sound, an attitude and an artistic vision that no one else could ever hope to match, and of course their music is as popular today as it was from the beginning. Witness The Beatles Anthology which came out in 1995 and the collection of their number one hits in 2001. The Beatles made more money in the past ten years than they made in all the years they were together, times ten.

And 1969 also brought the equally bizarre "Paul is dead" rumor that swept around the world almost overnight. They said it all started when a DJ in Detroit said over the air that he had received an anonymous phone call that Paul McCartney was dead. Within days the story took a life of its own. Before too long there was a frenzy of speculation that can only be described as macabre. Remember, how the rear cover photo of Abbey Road was supposed to symbolize a funeral procession? Or how people started playing Beatles albums backwards to pick up so-called clues? Pretty soon there was wide-spread belief that Paul had supposedly been killed in a car wreck a couple of years before, and that The Beatles were involved in an elaborate plot to cover it up. It was sheer madness is what it was. Of course, the record companies, Capitol in the U.S. and Apple in England, tried desperately to get The Beatles to issue a statement on film that it was all nonsense. But I think The Beatles new manager, the very bodacious and controversial Allen Klein, told each of them to lay low because of all the PR and spike in record sales. Don't ask me how but he must have thought the story was good for their career. Paul was secluded on his Scottish farm recording his first solo album and didn't want to be disturbed by a lot of nonsense. He was also said to be reeling with disgust over the spectacle that John and Yoko were making of themselves with their Bed-In for Peace, their strange art exhibits, and a host of odd causes they took up. He was also saddened by John's addiction to heroin.

Finally, Paul was tracked down by a photo team from Life magazine up at his farm, which is called High Park, and he still owns it. He was furious that his privacy had been breached and he threw a temper tantrum which included dousing them with a bucket of water. Well, all of this had been photographed and Paul, after realizing what he had done, negotiated a deal with them. They give him all their film and he'd give them an exclusive interview. Here's a copy of that issue:

Item-Fourteen—A copy of Dec 1969 *Life magazine*

Incidentally, the story that ran in here includes photos of his baby daughter taken by none other than Linda, the photographer, who of course I presume you all know died of cancer several years ago. A few days later Paul issued a statement saying, like Mark Twain, "The rumors of my death have been greatly exaggerated." Then he added, "However, if I was dead I'm sure I'd be the last to know." Nineteen hundred and seventy brought an official end to The Beatles as a group. By that time, it was a bizarre closing of an amazing story. Me, I was a fly on the wall, a butterfly really, who fluttered in then out, and even though I was always there close at hand, you'll barley read my name in any of the hundreds of books about them. That's because nobody close to them has every really told their story. And there are precious few around who still can. That's ultimately why I chose to confide in you. No splashy headlines here. No gossip, no mudslinging. For me it's all about the love I felt. I guess being around all those hippies actually rubbed off on me. They were right, of course, all you need is love.

Alf stands

This old box has been the keeper of these memories, and many more. I'm not sure what I should do with it now. I could sell it all, if anyone wants it. Remember I know all about Ebay now. And maybe I'll just hang on to it and pass it along to my son. I haven't decided yet. You see, in the end, everything about The Beatles that those of us who were close to them experienced, were actually quite personal experiences. I've tried to share some of these events with you. But what I can't share is the part that's in here.

He taps his chest.

And I think it's a large part. As big as this story is, it's still just the story of how those four lads became those four men. What a story it is too. All those years ago.

Thank you for listening. I bid you all hale well and farewell.

Alf bows and exits.

Lights out except for single spot on the now empty open box.

THE END

It Should Happen to You

It Should Happen to You

**A New York City art gallery owner seeks out
a new talent in rural America**

TIME: Spring 1969

PLACE: Scene One An upscale modern art gallery in New York City.

Scene Two A rural farmhouse in Fayetteville, Arkansas.

Scene Three The art gallery in New York City.

CHARACTERS:

Andrew Crispo: Age fortyish trendy but business-minded, owner of a well-regarded modern art gallery; pensive, frustrated.

Dirk Hamilton: Age mid-twentyish, gallery assistant; friendly, eater, earnest.

Stanley Freemont: Age mid-sixtyish or older folk artist; slightly doddering, forgetful; decidedly unambitious.

Jewel Freemont: Age mid-sixtyish, wife of Stanley; hospitable, sensible, folksy.

AT OPENING: Curtain opens on the Andrew Crispo Gallery above 57th Street in N.Y.C. The current exhibition is decidedly modernistic, not clearly evident as art at all. Beneath a white wall hang abstract expressionist paintings. There is a modern style desk and chair, modern for the era of the 1960's. Andrew Crispo is sitting at the desk looking at photographic slides against a floodlight in the ceiling. It is obvious he is not impressed by what he is viewing. An elderly couple enters to inspect the art but it is similarly evident they don't have a taste for modern art and they exit without saying a word to Crispo. He courteously nods farewell to them and after they exit says, sarcastically:

*   *   *

SCENE ONE

Andrew

Do come again!

He stands up and throws the remaining slides in his hand on the desktop.

Christ, how the hell am I supposed to make a buck selling this shit? Whoever came up with this idea of modern art anyway?

He looks at one of the paintings on his wall and then tips his head to the left and then slowly to the right, trying to make some sense of it.

It's a swindle I tell ya, a bold and audacious swindle!

Sooner or later this balloon is going to burst in all of our faces. And to think I wrote my master's thesis on the Pre-Raphaelites. Hmph!

His assistant Dirk Hamilton enters excitedly.

Dirk

Andrew great news! I think I've finally located Freemont. You were right he's in north central Arkansas. Faytteville to be exact, home of the University of Arkansas Razorbacks.

He hands Crispo a piece of paper, Crispo studies it.

Andrew

Rural Route 202, Boxtree County Road. Amazing; good work Dirk. I would have guessed southern Arkansas or maybe northern Mississippi, but Faytteville is good. Lots of southern history and culture there. And I once met a professor there from U of A, I can't remember where? It was a seminar about five years ago, Baltimore, yes in Baltimore. He was an émigré from Romania. He slipped away in Florence and he told me the communists back home tried him in abstentia and issued a death sentence because he supposedly took some antiquities with him. What was his name? Oh I can't think of it.

Dirk

maybe you could look him up when you're down there.

Andrew

Yes, that's a very good idea. How big could the art history department there be? He's probably still there too. I wonder if he ever get his wife and kids out? Hmph. I wonder.

Dirk

I'll see if I can look him up. Romanians have pretty distinct names. His will probably stick out like a sore thumb.

Andrew

Good idea Dirko, you do that. It's always good to renew old acquaintances. You never know when they might come in handy.

Dirk

Right, I'm on top of it.

Andrew

In the meantime Dirk we gotta do something and fast. This stuff isn't selling and the rent is going to double next month. We need an ace in the hold. And I think this man Freemont could be our savior. His work is so authentic and so immutably American! I believe he could be the next Thomas Hart Benton. We just have to get our hands on him first.

Dirk

Well, now that we have his address we can send him a letter and ask him if he'd like to see you.

Andrew

Yeah, from the looks of his address I doubt he has a telephone. maybe I should just pop in on him and play it by ear. I can always say I was just down there visiting the Romanian.

Dirk

Could do. I checked the airlines. You can take Southern Air from LaGuardia to Memphis and then a connecting flight to Little Rock. You'll have to rent a car from there. It's a three-hour drive to Faytteville from there.

Andrew

Tell you what Mr. Dirk; let's get a letter to him this afternoon. Instead of flying I think I'll drive down so I have my convertible with me. It's bound to be awfully muggy there this time of year. That way I can take my time and explore a bit while I am down there. I like the idea of the south. The Confederacy is long gone it's true but I have a feeling there are a few remnants that have survived. I'd like to see if I can find them. After all, one thing is certain, even vanquished civilizations yearn to prove they once existed.

Dirk

Well said boss. It's only been a hundred and five years. There's bound to be some tell-tale signs here and there. In fact, I think that might be a good idea for an article for The Times Art and Travel section. You'll definitely need to take your camera with you. You never know things that people have taken for granted for years could pop out at you like, like…

Andrew

Like Satan in the pulpit. You're probably right Dirko. Good thinking! Well let's get this letter together. We'll post it tomorrow. I'll head out Sunday. He'll probably get it by the middle of next week.

Dirk

Assuming that rural route has daily delivery.

Andrew

Right, but either way it'll take me at least three days of driving time, because I don't want to overdo it. He should get the letter by the time I arrive. God I hope nobody else is courting him. Wouldn't that be ironic!

Dirk

Don't worry yourself over it. If it was meant to be that you'd be his exclusive dealer, then it'll happen. If not, well then c'est la vie.

Andrew

Don't say that Dirko, we need Freemont more than he needs us. Why can't we find the artist equivalent of The Beatles? Is Liverpool any more promising than Faytteville? I doubt it. Besides, what we need are American artists, not cranky British or German ones.

Dirk

And think of the savings in shipping and customs costs too!

Andrew

Exactly, now you're thinking like a real businessman. I have a good feeling about this guy Dirk. He just might be the one we've been looking for.

Dirk

And just think, he's probably dying to hear from us. What artist wouldn't be?

Andrew

You know, I'll bet you're right, he probably is.

Dirk

Okay let me oil up the typewriter. Start drafting a letter while I finish up your thank you note to Mrs. Fleming.

Andrew

Yes, good idea. That's the last sale we had. Okay, go to it.

Another couple enters the art gallery as Dirk exits….Andrew gestures to them in a welcoming manner.

Please do come in. This is the work of the best artist to come out of Germany that is not overtly political.

They both inspect the art furtively and quickly, then leave without a word.

Great, just fucking great. Fucking Germans!

Andrew

He picks up a pad of paper and pencil swivels his seat around so his back is to the audience and says to the pad.

"Dear Mr. Freemont…."

No, "My Dear Mr. Freemont…."

End of Scene One

SCENE TWO

Setting: The living room gallery of Stanley Freemont's home. Canvases cover every square foot of the walls and only a single table with two chairs is unencumbered with paintings or supplies. An art easel and stool are placed in front of the room's only window. Freemont is seated at the easel with a brush in his hand but he is staring out of the window in a daydream.

Time: One week later.

Knocks on the front door. Freemont is slightly startled but doesn't move. His wife Jewel enters with a dishtowel in hand.

Jewel

I wonder who that could be? I sure hope it ain't that travelin' salesman again. Seems he stops by more and more all the time. Don't he know that we ain't buyin'?

Stanley

We sure ain't mother.

He never looks away from the window; she opens the door and is surprised to find Andrew, styrofoam cup in hand and smiling.

Jewel

Well who does we have here? A genuine stranger I reckon.

She opens the screen door and Andrew enters.
Can I help you stranger? You don't look like you're from around these parts. Where you from, Little Rock?

Andrew

Ah, no ma'am, I'm from New York City. Andrew Crispo is my name. Pleased to meet you.

He offers his hand but she doesn't accept it.

Jewel

Well Mr. Crispo, whatever it is you're sellin' we ain't buyin'. We got here just about everything we needs, ain't we Stanley?

Stanley

I should say so ma. The Lord has blessed us richly.

Jewel

Indeed he has. Amen to that!

Andrew

Yes, Amen to that! Certainly. But I'm not selling anything, so don't be alarmed.

He suddenly looks around the living room and is dumbstruck by what he sees.

My God! This is fantastic. I can see I am in the right place but I'll admit that I had a heck of a time finding it.

Jewel

And what might your business be Mr. Crispo? I ain't never heard anybody speak with an accent like ya'll got, 'cept maybe Walter Cronkite back before the television went on the fritz.

Andrew

Well I presume this is the residence of Mr. Stanley Freemont, the painter?

Jewel

You reckon right young man. There he is now but I don't think he's heard a word we have been speakin'.

Whispering.

He sleeps standin' up sometimes.

Stanley

Now mother, I'm perfectly wide awake, though I wish I weren't right about now. Strange dreams interrupted my sleep last night, I mean mostly this 'smorn, I reckon. But yes sir, I'm Stanley Freemont and it's a pleasure to meet ya. We ain't made it to New York City yet but we was thinking of catching the Greyhound from Faytteville. I've always had a mind about visiting the Metropolitan Museum there and seeing the Statue of a Liberty. maybe one day, maybe, maybe. Have a seat, friend.

Andrew

Thank you Mr. Freemont and thank you Mrs. Freemont. I can assure it is my pleasure to meet you both. I drove down here starting last Sunday but I experienced some mechanical trouble in Pennsylvania. That set me back two whole days. I wonder, did you receive my letter? From Arleen Crispo Gallery? No?

Jewel

We only get mail once per week, on Fridays so it may be here tomorra'. But now that you're here, why don't ya state yer business. We don't know nothin' bout no gallery if that's what you're seekin'. Ain't no gallery round here.

Stanley

There's a shootin' gallery two towns over if that's what you're after. A hunter are ya Mr. Crispo? Let me guess: Quail, Pheasant, even Turkey maybe?

Andrew

No, not me. I'm no hunter. At least not of living things. No I'm what you call "city folk". We don't do much hunting in New York. Central Park is about as rural as it gets in Manhattan.

Jewel

Well if you ain't selling' and you ain't shootin', then what are ya after? Can ya tell us that?

Andrew

He spreads his arms widely.

This! This is what I'm after, may I?

He begins looking and inspecting canvasses.

Your art work Mr. Freemont. I learned about you from a piece I saw on display at American Folk Art Exhibit on 52nd Street. You have a piece in that show, untitled, of a group of people, farmers I'm guessing, lining up waiting to square dance at their local grange hall. It's magnificent!

Jewel

Oh, you must mean that there paintin' from the senator's office. We gave that to thank him for getting our road paved a two, three years ago now.

Stanley

Yep, I remember it well.

Andrew

The painting?

Stanley

No, the pavin' crew. Loud as a freight train but they did a mighty might purdy job. You have no idea how muddy that ole road use to get after a shower. It was a mess and then some.

Jewel

Stanley gave the senator one of his paintins' as a thank you. I wonder how it got all the way to New York City. You don't think he gave it away or traded it or somethin', do ya?

Andrew

No, no, no. In fact it was a loan from his office. That's how I tracked you down. It was the senator's secretary that gave us your address. I don't take it you have a telephone, do you?

Jewel

Lord no.

Stanley

No telephone lines out here Mr. Crispo. That there senator of ours would get a second paintin' if he can arrange that. Yes sir, a telephone would be a great asset to these parts. They keep promisin' but ole ma Bell just 'tain't listenin' I guess.

Jewel

The nearest phone is at the Post Office in Baker City 'bout twenty-five miles south of here. A long way to go for a call. But Johnny Jenkins up the road was a radio-man during the war. He has a short wave radio set-up and we can get a word in and out through him if needs be.

Stanley

Yep, he's real friendly-like. An American hero too. He's in one of these paintins' around here somewhere, a talkin' on his radio. Thar, up thar. There ole Jonny is. Bless his soul.

Andrew

Did you serve in the war Mr. Freemont?

Stanley

Well no, I was called up when I was eighteen but….

Jewel

Then word came that his older brother Elsmer got killed in that training accident in Hawaia'. So they cancelled his induction because he was the only son left.

Stanley

I could've gone in but I didn't have the heart for it. I am an artist not a fighter. I'd rather draw than kill, if you know what I mean.

Andrew

Can't fault you for that. My sympathies for the loss of your brother. It must've been very hard. One of my uncles was wounded at Pearl Harbor. Who knows, maybe he knew your brother.

Jewel

Well would you imagine that, maybe he did, maybe he did.

Stanley

I suppose it's possible, them islands is mighty tiny I hear.

They all laugh.

Andrew

Well, let me get to the point of my visit. You see, I run an art gallery in the city and I am very much interested in offering you exclusive representation in the art world. This would give you an opportunity to sell some of your paintings and earn some money so you paint more. Or purchase a new T.V. or build onto the house to give yourself a big studio. I really love your work and believe you are immensely talented.

Stanley

Thank ya.

Jewel

Ain't that nice.

Andrew

And I believe that art world is hungry for work like this. Real art. Real stories made with painstaking skill but with a universal vision. I see a hint of Thomas Hart Benton, Norman Rockwell, and Grant Wood in your work, Mr. Freemont. I believe if we play our cards right, you'll probably become just as well-known, and just as successful as all three. What do you say to that?

Stanley

Well honestly I don't know Mr. Andrew. I, ah, never gave it no mind. You see paintin' for me ain't a job, it's a hobby. I only do it in my spare time.

Andrew

Well how do you earn a living out here?

Stanley

Well we don't need much. The house and land is all paid for and we don't have big appetites do we ma? Ha, ha.

Jewel

We own sixty-five acres down the road Mr. Andrew. We lease it out to farmers and they pay us a good rent. We ain't got a car because we don't drive.

Andrew

Do you have any children?

Jewel

We do. Our son is in Baker City running a dairy rig farm to farm collecting milk. If we needs to get somewhere, he drives us. And we have twin daughters both of whom are married and livin' near Faytteville. No grandchildren yet. Soon I reckon. They say they is workin' on it.

She shows him framed family photos.

Andrew

I see, well what do you say to my proposal? We'll have a big exhibition. With as many canvasses it'll be the talk of the town. Why you'll be at the top of the Statue of Liberty sooner than you can blink an eye. What'd you say?

Stanley

Well it's real flatterin' Mr. Andrew, but I don't know. I have a hard time partin' with my paintins' and when I do I usually give them away.

Andrew

I don't know why you should feel that way. On my way here a few miles up the road I saw a sign out front of a house selling handmade rocking chairs. I imagine there's plenty of folks in this country who sell what they make. It's the good old American way. It's commerce, it's industry.

Stanley

I reckon you're right Mr. Andrew but paintins and art works ain't in the same category as rockin' chairs or tables or bookshelves. Those are useful! How the heck can I accept money for something that'll just be gathering dust on a wall? It just don't seem right. I makes 'em because it's in me not because I wants to sell 'em for money.

Jewel

Excuse my manners Mr. Andrew, I haven't offered you anything to eat or drink. Is you hungry at all? We don't usually make much of lunchtime but I could surely fix you a salad and a sandwich. What'd ya say?

Andrew

Thanks that would be great! A glass of cold water would be great too.

Stanley

As long as you don't mind well water, we can handle that. Our well is old but reliable!

Jewel

Amen to that. I'll be right back. You just make yourself right 'cheer at home. I do wish you would've brought Mrs. Andrew with ya! Such a shame, we don't often get no out of town visitors. Certainly not from New York City. 'Scuse me now.

She exits.

Andrew

He begins to walk around to view the numerous paintings all around him.

I guess I understand your feelings Stanley. I may call you Stanley?

Freemont nods.

I once knew a very fine artist, who couldn't bear to part with his work because he felt each piece was kinda like his own child.

Stanley

makes sense.

Andrew

Yes, I suppose to some it might. But a man's gotta eat Stanley. If you know what I mean.

Stanley

Pats his belly.

I sure does, he he. We eats just fine 'round here. Praise the Lord!

Andrew

Yes indeed.

Struggling for words.

Ah, you see Stanley, a small canvas like this could bring you maybe, two or three thousand dollars. That's a lot of money.

Stanley

It sure is. Dang!

Stanley takes the painting from him.

You don't say. Two or three thousand. Dang! This one here is about five or six years old. Still a kid.

Andrew

It's a very fine piece. I'd love to show it at my gallery. It'd be an honor.

Stanley

No, the honor would be mine I'm sure but I'm gonna have to decline your offer. I'd feel funny about puttin' up my paintins in New York City. Hell I won't even put 'em up at the grange hall. No, they're doing just fine right 'cheer at home. Besides, it'd be an awful lot of fuss to move 'em.

Andrew

No, No I'd handle all of that. I'd send a truck down with a couple of men. We'd take care of everything. Heck it'd give you an opportunity to put a fresh coat of paint on your walls.

Stanley

Yeah, maybe you is right. I didn't think of that.

Pause.

But naw, I'm happy the way things are. I don't like stirring up the pot, if you know what I mean.

Andrew

No really Stanley. Ah, think of your family. Wouldn't it be nice to earn some money for your children and your grandchildren? It's not easy to save nowadays you know. You could put everything you earn in a savings account for them.

Stanley

Yes, that's true I suppose. But they'll have to look out for themselves I figure.

Jewel re-enters with a tray.

Jewel

Here we go Mr. Andrew, a nice cold glass of water and a sandwich with some fresh home grown vegetables for ya on the side.

Andrew

Thank you very much Mrs. Freemont.

He tastes the water but quickly finds it is not to his liking.

Ooo wee. Now that's what I call well water.

They all laugh...

Mrs. Freemont, Stanley here seems to believe his paintings aren't worthy of going to New York and being exhibited for sale in my gallery. He's much too modest, don't you agree? He's brilliant and his work deserves to be seen and appreciated!

Jewel

Well, that's just the way he is. There was a professor who came by about a year and a half ago, spoke with a really funny accent like I never have heard before. Said he was, from the college over in Fayetteville. Said he heard about Stanley's paintins' from a farmer who supplies eggs and cheese to the school there. Said Stanley's paintin' was called Folk Art because Stanley ain't never had no formal trainin' in art workin'. Said he wanted to make a showing of folky art from around the state. Remember him Stanley?

Stanley

Now that you mention him, I does. He said he was from Romania or somethin' like that. Could pert barely make out a word from him. He even left his card here somewhere.

He looks on a table next to his easel.

Why it's right cheer: "Alexander Tar-an-es-que." I think that's a it. Here you can have it if you like. Don't do me no good.

He hands Andrew the card.

Andrew

Alexander Tarenecue, yes. maybe I'll give him a ring. We probably have a few things in common. But surely you'll reconsider Stanley. You have no reason to feel bashful. I can assure you, I'd consider it to be an honor to be your agent. In a couple years I'll have your work in some very prestigious private collections. Then after that, we'll pitch it to some important museums. I dare say the art institute in Little Rock would be proud to own one of your paintings.

Jewel

Oh, they got one a few years ago Mr. Andrew. We donated it to them for an auction but they didn't sell it.

Stanley

maybe nobody bid on it.

Andrew

Or maybe they thought it was too good to part with and they kept it. It could be on exhibition as we speak, did you ever think of that?

Stanley

Can't say that I have. Wouldn't that be somethin' ma?

Jewel

Sure would. Next time we go down there, we should visit that there museum. We always wanted to. Didn't we Stanley?

Stanley

I should say so, now maybe we have a good reason to make the trip.

Andrew

Yes you do, why I'd drive you there myself.

Jewel

Oh that's real kind of you Mr. Andrew but we could manage that on our own. My sister and her family lives in North Little Rock. We were planin' on visitin' her in November fer Thanksgivin'. That'd be a good time to visit the museum, wouldn't it be Stanley? Wouldn't it?

Stanley

Whatever you say ma.

Andrew

Sounds like a plan Mrs. Freemont, don't you believe your husband's art deserves a wider audience? I mean after all, it certainly would mean a lot more income for your household. Hell you could purchase another fifty acres of land here for maybe four or five paintings. You'd like that wouldn't you?

Jewel

It ain't up to me, no siree. It sure ain't. Stanley makes 'em, frames 'em and all. If he don't wants to part with 'em there ain't a thing I can say or do to change his mind. Right Stanley?

Stanley

If you say so ma.

Andrew

But surely you have more than enough paintings here to keep you happy. And you can always create more. What there must be fifty or sixty pieces here, maybe more. Why you're looking at maybe a million dollars on them walls alone. Did you hear, that's a million dollars?

Jewel

Plus you ain't seen what's in the barn neither.

Andrew

More yet? My word. You have been busy, huh Stanley?

Stanley

But I'm slowin' down some. My eyes ain't a workin' good and my wrist and elbow been givin' me aches worse and worse. Old age I reckon.

Andrew

Still Stanley, you've got a real legacy here. It'd be a shame not to share it with the world. After all where would you be if Picasso or Matisse kept their artwork all to themselves? It'd be a terrible shame.

Stanley

I reckon you're right. But lookee here, those fellas was born to be artists. Me, I just picked it up along the way. I started as a sign painter and then I painted some barns and also some billboards out on Route 15. I had some left over paint from the highway jobs that I just put it to use on these here country scenes. It ain't art, it's closer to whittlin' really! Some things just ain't made fer sellin' I figure.

Jewel

Amen to that Stanley. Remember what the Lord said 'bout temptation. The road to damnation is the very next exit. When Stanley is moved by the Almighty to sell or donate his paintins', he'll recognize the sign He sends. Until then we'll just keep 'em here, safe and ready for his callin'.

Stanley

Well said mother!

Andrew

Surely the Lord won't miss a dozen or two paintings. Or you could always sell them and donate the proceeds to your church.

Stanley

Like I said Mr. Andrew some things just ain't made fer sellin'.

Jewel

Go on and have our lunch Mr. Andrew. Then afterwards I'll take ya out to the garden and you can pick some cukes and peppers and tomatoes to take home to Mrs. Andrew. Oh and the cabbage this year is hard as boulders. Heavy as 'em too.

Andrew

Thanks Mrs. Freemont.

He reluctantly takes a bite of the sandwich. With his mouthful he says:
I just love a good hard cabbage.

End of Scene Two

SCENE THREE

Setting: The Andrew Crispo Gallery in New York City.

Time: Eight days later.

Andrew enters carrying the same painting he held at Freemont's house. He looks at it admiringly and then places it on the easel next to his desk. He flips thru a week's worth of mail.

Andrew

Bill, bill, bill, ah, Mr. & Mrs. Stanley Freemont.

He opens the letter; it is a hand-painted thank you card. He reads:

"Dear Mr. Crispo, Stanley and I wish to thank you for your visit and kind invitation to exhibit in your gallery. After giving the matter some thought *(his voice rising, sounding hopeful)* we have decided that Stanley's paintings were created for our home and that's where the Lord wants them to stay. If circumstances change, you will be the first person we call. And at that time we will accept your offer to host us in New York City. Our kindly regards, Jewel & Stanley Freemont. P.S. I hope you saved some of our tomatoes for the missus."

He drops the note on his desk.

Well I suppose that's the proverbial opening of the door. Mission semi-accomplished.

Dirk enters enthusiastically.

Dirk

Andrew, welcome home, well, tell me how did it go?

Andrew

It went.

Dirk

What do you mean? What happened? Did you sign him up?

He spots the Freemont painting.

Oh, my God! You brought one home. It's excellent. The guy definitely has talent. It has everything. Very rich, very rich indeed.

Andrew

Yes, color, light, composition, artistic flair, and vision. Everything!

Dirk

Well? Tell me.

Andrew

I struck out.

Dirk

What?

Andrew

I struck out. He threw me a curveball and I whiffed!

Dirk

What do you mean you whiffed?

Andrew

I mean I couldn't get through to him. He doesn't want to sell his art. He'll give it away or trade it for something but he refuses to sell it. He doesn't think that's the way it was meant to be or something like that.

Dirk

What, that's crazy!

Andrew

You should have seen his home. In the sticks but comfy none-theless. His studio takes up the whole living room. Paintings in every square inch of wall and more leaning against furniture and stacked up three and four high. Plus there's even more in the barn. I'm guessing another hundred pieces. And some of them are very big and absolutely gorgeous. It's a crying shame I tell you. He's everything we've been looking for. A meal ticket you can feel good about peddling.

Dirk

No kidding. maybe he didn't understand exactly what you had in mind.

Andrew

Oh, he understood just fine. Here, read this card I just opened. It's from Mrs. Freemont, his spokesperson, manager and book-ing agent.

He hands it to Dirk.

Dirk

Wow, this card is hand-painted, It's beautiful a garden patch.

Andrew

With hard and heavy cabbages!

Dirk reads it.

Dirk

I see. Well maybe he'll reconsider if we stay in touch. We should send them a gift. Something they really need.

Andrew

A television! Great idea. And we'll get them a colored one too. They'll love it.

Dirk

Well you got one piece out of them. How much does he want for this?

Andrew

No that's a gift they gave me. They were very kind, very sweet people. Country bumpkins you know. Not dumb but kind of simple. In a good way.

Dirk

Well perhaps we can sell it to Mrs. Cummings or to Metro Tech for their collection. We can tell them quite honestly it's a really rare piece.

Andrew

You know Dirko. I think I'm going to keep it. I think it's going to grow on me. It has sentimental value to me now. Besides Dirk, as an art dealer you should know some things just ain't made fer' sellin'.

They both admire the painting.

Dirk

I see. Yes, I see!

End of Scene Three

THE END

Bluesman Brando

Bluesman Brando

**The temperamental movie star bonds with
a suburban family as he pursues an invention
to augment the sound of a harmonica—
the blues harp as he prefers to call it**

TIME:	Autumn 1979
PLACE:	Sherman Oaks, California
SETTING:	The living room and kitchen of a modern suburban home.

CHARACTERS:

Anthony Carlin: Ordinary middle-aged product design engineer

Tammy Carlin: *His 12-year-old autistic daughter*

Linda Carlin: (voice only) Anthony's wife

Arthur Hoffman: (voice only) Brando's manager

Marlon Brando: At age 55, six years after *The Godfather*

AT OPENING: Anthony Carlin is busy straightening up his living room in obvious anticipation of receiving a guest. He then crosses to the kitchen and clears the table of breakfast clutter. He accidentally knocks over a box of Cheerios and they spill all over the floor.

*   *   *

Anthony

Damn!

He grabs a broom and dustpan.

Frickin' Cheerios!

He sweeps up the mess and deposits the sweepings into a trash bin.

Frickin' Cheerios!

He then peers into the box and shakes it to determine its remaining contents.

Damn, this is the last box!

He continues to clean the kitchen.

Tammy

Voice only from stage right bedroom.

Daddy?

Anthony

Yes, honey?

Tammy

Did you know that baboons live the longest of all primates?

Anthony

I had no idea honey. That's nice. Keep studying. "B" is a particularly excellent letter of the alphabet, one of my two or three favorites.

Tammy

Okay, but just until mommy gets home. Then we are going shopping for a birthday present for Brittany.

Anthony

Well, hopefully your mom is not too tired to take you.

Tammy

She promised.

Anthony

Okay then, good. Tell me another interesting thing about baboons. Where is their habitat. What is their favorite food?

The telephone rings. Anthony answers it.

Hello? Hi. What's up? *He listens for a moment.* Emergency Room emergency earthquake drill training? This morning? All day? Oh, Linda, not today, not of all days. Can you get out of it? All supervisors are mandatory personnel. I see. And what am I supposed to do with her when he gets here? Tell me that. *He listens.* Can we call Brittany's mom? No. Anybody? I'm not making a big deal out of it, but this is a big deal. It's not every day that Marlon Brando comes over! *He listens.* So that's your solution, give her a box of Cheerios and a dictionary. That's it? Can I lock her in her room? Okay, okay. I won't. Geez, relax. So, when will you be finished? No idea. Are you at least getting overtime pay? You better be or there will be an emergency over there. *He listens.* And what am I supposed to tell her royal highness about not going shopping with you this morning? Um hum. Sure, she'll understand. She's a big girl. Oh sure. I'm exaggerating. I'm being melodramatic. I have nothing to fear. Nothing at all. It's all in my head.

Anthony continues.

Hold on a second while I tell her, I don't want you to miss any of the fireworks. Tammy darling, it's your mom on the phone. She has to work overtime and can't take you shopping this morning. *There is an immediate loud bone-chilling shriek of horror, followed by a wailing of grief-stricken crying.* I trust I've made my point once again. Slam dunk. I'm right, you're wrong, once again…again! *He listens intently.* Oh, now you have to go. Let me guess, it's an emergency. How convenient! Save a blood transfusion for me. Bye! *He hangs up the phone as the crying intensifies.* Frickin' great! Of all the days of the year. *He yells toward the bedroom.* Honey, after my meeting, I'll take you shopping myself, okay?

Tammy

Voice only. No! She promised.

Anthony

I know she promised. She knows she promised, but does it really have to be this morning? Can't it wait until this afternoon?

Tammy

No!

Anthony

Well, I'm sorry sweetheart. It'll have to wait. Things came up. Life is full of surprises. We all have to learn to deal with them. Remember what your mom was telling you about maturity?

Tammy

About tampons?

Anthony

No, that was puberty. I'm talking about maturity, you know. About acting your age. Behaving yourself.

Tammy

No!

Anthony

Okay, suit yourself. *She starts crying again.* The phone rings. He answers it. Hello? Ah, Mr. Hoffman, good to hear from you. Are we still on for this morning? I'm all ready for him.

Hoffman

Voice only. Good morning Tony. Yeah, we're still on. I'm just checking in with you to make sure you are ready and understand all the ground rules and everything.

Anthony

I understand entirely. Stick to the task at hand. Don't ask any questions about his movies. No autographs. No photographs. Everything is strictly confidential.

Hoffman

That's right, good. You are alone, aren't you? Privacy is paramount to him. That's why he doesn't want to meet in your office.

Anthony

I understand entirely. It's my pleasure. No problem at all. *Tammy wails a scream of frustration. Anthony attempts to muffle the phone.*

Hoffman

What was that?

Anthony

Uh, I accidentally stepped on my cat's tail. She's a sensitive old girl. He's not allergic to cats is he?

Hoffman

That is a good question. I honestly don't know. Delores, is Brando allergic to cats? No, good. No, he's not, but you better get rid of it just in case. Can you put her outside or in a bedroom?

Anthony

Yeah, I think I'll lock her up in her bedroom. I mean my bedroom. No problem. Is there anything else?

Hoffman

Just remember that this project is his baby. He's very passionate about it. So do a good job for him. You can discuss all the details with him. When you need a check I'll send it to you. That's the kind of thing a personal manager does for his clients.

Anthony

I understand. I wish I had one myself.

Hoffman

You do. It's called a wife! *They both laugh.* And I've got one too.

Hoffman continues.

Do you have any other questions?

Anthony

No, I can't think of any. We should be fine. I promise he'll come away from this meeting with a lot of information and answers about this invention of his.

Hoffman

Good, that's what we want. You come well-recommended. That's why we chose you.

Anthony

Thank you, I appreciate that. If it can be done, I'll get it done. That's my motto.

Hoffman

Sounds good to me. And one last thing, Tony. I just want to advise you a word of caution if you will.

Anthony

Yeah, what's that?

Hoffman

Well, he's a bit of a cheapskate. Tight-fisted to the bare knuckles. Whatever price you give him, he'll complain about and bargain you down. Let him feel he's getting the best of you, like you're doing him a big favor. So start higher then you need to so you can come down some. He needs to feel he's getting a really good deal.

Anthony

I understand entirely. He want's my first-cousin rate. Not a problem. Thanks for the heads-up.

Hoffmann

Okay then. He's very punctual, so he'll be there exactly at 9 a.m. Good luck and call me when you're finished and brief me on how it went, okay?

Anthony

Okay, Mr. Hoffman. I will. Thanks for calling. You've been really helpful.

Hoffman

Good luck then. Bye for now.

Anthony

Thanks again, bye.

He hangs up the phone. He tip-toes to stage right to listen carefully to any more crying from his daughter. He believes she has cried herself to sleep and crosses both his fingers in a gesture of hopeful luck. He tip-toes away and surveys the house in one final inspection.

Tammy

Voice only. I want Cheerios!

Anthony

He slaps his brow in disappointment. Coming. He grabs the nearly empty box and exits stage right to take it to her. He re-enters. You better go easy on them honey. That's the last box. Did you find the answers to my questions about baboons?

Tammy

I'm past that daddy. I'm reading about babies now.

Anthony

That's nice. Babies are nice. Take your time. And remember, take notes too.

He plops down on the sofa for a respite. A moment later, the doorbell rings. He jumps up to answer it, but not before first once again tip-toeing stage right to listen for any more sounds from his daughter's bedroom. He takes a deep breath, collects himself and opens the door.

In the background, Tammy's voice is heard reading a list of words that begin with the letter B, starting with "Baby." She continues reading from the list for the next several minutes, the audio level going up and down as needed to keep her pesky presence in Anthony's mind. A list of the "B" words is provided at the end of the play.

Come in Mr. Brando. You're actually a little early.

Brando

Thank you. The morning traffic wasn't as bad as I feared it would be.

Anthony

Did you drive yourself?

Brando

Oh sure. I drive everywhere myself. Chauffeurs are too expensive and taxis are a pain in the ass.

Anthony

You're telling me, especially when you're stuck in these valley traffic jams, you can get murdered in just ten miles. Please come in. Let me have your hat. I see you have your plans.

Brando

Raises the blueprint tube he is carrying. Absolutely. For your eyes only.

Anthony

Would you like to sit here and talk first, or do you want to go over the prints on the kitchen table now?

Brando

Let's do both at the table.

As he walks in the kitchen, Brando stops, looks puzzled, sniffs around conspicuously, and turns to Anthony.

Anthony

Is anything wrong?

Brando

Cheerios! I smell Cheerios. I haven't smelled Cheerios in more than fifty years. No, more than sixty years. Isn't that amazing I can still remember that smell?

Anthony

Yes, that is amazing. Truly amazing. We had Cheerios for breakfast.

Brando

Who is we?

Anthony

Umm, um, my daughter and I.

Brando

Oh, you have a daughter? What's her name? How old is she?

Anthony

Yes, just one thank God. Her name is Tammy and she is 12. Please take a seat.

Brando

That's very nice. Twelve years old. She's a young lady.

Anthony

Well, soon. Not yet. She's autistic so she's developing, slowly. If you know what I mean.

Brando

I know exactly what you mean. My youngest son is autistic too. It's hell. His mother is a saint. I don't know how she puts up with him. I've never told anybody this, but that's why I left her. I wanted her to focus all her energies on him and not me. It would have been unfair of me to soak up all her love and caring, when he needs it so much more than I do.

Anthony

Wow, that's very … interesting. *An awkward pause ensues.* Can I get you anything to drink? Coffee or tea or orange juice?

To Tammy in her bedroom: Not so loud honey.

Brando

Do you have any pineapple juice? I only drink pineapple juice.

Anthony

No, I'm sorry; no pineapple juice. We pretty much only buy what Tammy drinks and she likes orange juice, Pulp-free of course.

Brando

Of course. I understand completely. You give 'em OJ with pulp and you might as well forget the rest of the day. They'll never let you forget it. Trust me, I've been there.

Anthony

I can see you have.

Brando

Is she off at school?

Anthony

Ah, no. School is on vacation this week. She's taking a nap right now. Don't worry, she won't distract us.

Tammy

Voice only. Daddy! We're out of Cheerios!

Anthony

Excuse me a moment.

Brando

Take your time.

Anthony exits and quickly re-enters.

Anthony

She is obsessed with Cheerios. That's why you could smell them. I knocked over a whole box while I was cleaning up and we don't have any more.

Brando

It's okay. I understand completely. Don't sweat it. My son is obsessed with chili peppers. Can you imagine that? Chili peppers of all things. And the hotter the pepper, the better. And I don't even know how it started. One day he demanded chili peppers and he hasn't stopped since. He's 17 now. And before chili peppers, it was gold and silver. He was crazy about pirate's treasure chests. I had to buy him all of this gaudy costume jewelry and stuff that looked like doubloons and pieces of eight. And I found an old movie prop treasure chest for him. He drove us crazy. What is it about these kids?

Anthony

Don't ask me. They're a blessing and a curse. All children are but these in particular much more so.

Brando

It's true. Even my daughter. Normal as can be, but still a pain in the ass most of the time.

Anthony

But where would you be without them?

Brando

In Tahiti that's where!

Anthony

Tahiti?

Brando

Yeah, I own an island there. I love it, but it is so remote, it is hard to get there and enjoy it. There's no telephone service. Only short-wave radio. That's where I learned to love pineapple juice. It's our native drink there.

Anthony

Wow! Why Tahiti?

Brando

I fell in love with it when I made *Mutiny on the Bounty* back in '62. Crazy I know. It's been my own obsession in a way. But I love it. I'm gonna be buried there and my grave marker is going to be a royal palm tree and nothing else.

Anthony

Wow! Sounds great!

Brando

Yeah, but with my luck, it'll probably grow crooked. Hah! What about a wife? You got one of those too.

Anthony

Indeed, I do. A good one too.

Brando

Glad to hear it.

Anthony

She's an emergency room nurse. In fact, a few months ago, she was made supervisor.

Brando

Congratulations!

Anthony

She works the graveyard shift and normally she is home by now, but she called a little while ago to tell me they are having an emergency room emergency earthquake drill. She has to work today as well. That's why I got stuck with Tammy instead of being alone as we agreed.

Brando

It's quite okay. I don't mind it at all. I'm not as big an ass as they say I am. You know how the press likes to exaggerate things like that.

Anthony

Right. Okay, so let's see what you've got here.

Brando

An emergency room nurse, huh? That must be very convenient if you are choking on an olive pit or something. Or, if somebody stabs you in the back at a restaurant. It can happen you know.

Anthony

Right. I suppose it can.

Brando

Fans can be crazier than criminals, believe me. I know.

Anthony

I believe you.

Brando

An ER nurse would be very handy on Tahiti. Very handy indeed.

Anthony

I'll bet. So, getting back to your project here…I'm curious to know about when you started to play the harmonica.

Brando

It's not a harmonica. I play the blues harp. It's a little different than a harmonica.

Anthony

Oh, kind of like a violin and a fiddle?

Brando

Yeah, that's right. A good analogy. I like that. You're a good thinker I can tell.

Anthony

Oh, I don't know. I'm just a tool and die man. I work with my hands more than my brains.

Brando

I started playing blues harp when I started making movies in the early '50s. There is so much dead time on a film set. Most actors are busy learning their lines. But I never had a problem memorizing my lines, so I took up the blues harp to pass the time because I've always been into the blues. It was more convenient than lugging around an electric guitar.

Anthony

I'll bet.

Brando

So, I eventually got pretty good at it. You know, on the set of *A Street Car Named Desire*, I had my blues harp in my pocket in every scene. It kind of became my good luck charm ever since.

Anthony

Wow! You'll never believe it, but my parents named my younger sister Vivian Leigh Carlin because of that movie. Or maybe because of *Gone with the Wind*, I'm not sure. *Awkward pause*. So, you carried a harmonica in…

Brando

Not harmonica. Blues harp!

Anthony

I mean blues harp, in your pocket on all your movies?

Brando

That's right. Every one. One time, during the making of *Guys and Dolls*, I had this romantic scene with Jean Simmons, who was supposed to be sloshed in a Havana night club. She was very shy and proper, so the director wanted to loosen her up a bit, so he asked her to drink some rum and cokes. She wouldn't do it unless I agreed to as well. So I said, what the hell. Sure. So we got sloshed to do the scene. In one part, when we are dancing real

close, I put the blues harp in my shorts so it felt like a boner. She
freaked out, but never lost character. I never had the guts to tell
her the truth. She probably really thought I got a hard-on for her,
when in fact, I always thought she was a real zero. But she was a
good actress and easy to work opposite of. And she had nice tits.
That's always a plus.

Anthony

Wow, that's funny. You could tell that one on *The Tonight Show*.
Carson would love it.

Brando

Yeah, I'll bet he would.

Anthony

Well, let's get down to business before you-know-who steals center stage.

He peers at the drawings rolled out on the kitchen table.

I can see you got some real professionals to spec this all out. A
hand-held mini microphone especially for blues harp players.

Brando

You have to understand the basic concept. For years, harpists
have had to blow into standard mikes and it is both awkward and
uncomfortable. So, I figured it would be a good idea to design a
microphone especially for our needs. So, I came up with this. I call
it The Butterfly, because it is shaped kind of like a cocoon, but that
would be a lousy name. Butterfly is better.

Anthony

And more marketable.

Brando

Thank you. So you see how it fits on the middle and ring finger of your verso hand. That's the hand that isn't holding the harp, but allows you to play effects. Like this.

He shows Anthony by pretending to play.

Anthony

I understand. Let's see your list of materials. That'll be the key for how long this will take me to do. He selects another sheet. I see. A steel housing with molded rubber cavities. Extruded plastic mount pad. Aluminum finger ring. This seems fine, but it is going to take me a few days to estimate the cost.

Brando

That's fine. Any ideas about the range?

Anthony

You want a dozen prototypes, right?

Brando

At least a dozen, or even two dozen.

Anthony

Well, the real cost is in the first one. Every one after that, is just material and bench work. Pretty minimal. Do you want us to fit the microphone or the mike manufacturer?

Brando

What do you think?

Anthony

We can do it if you can supply us. Or we can just make the housing and let them fit it. It's their call really. It's their baby. Their mike, we're just making the mike stand.

Brando

Yeah, I like that. It is like a mike stand, but for the hand. I might use that as a slogan. Can I?

Anthony

Absolutely!

Brando

So what about a cost range? Any ideas? Just so I have some idea. You gotta be good to me because I'm not taking bids. You're it.

Anthony

The one-time costs like the die and jigs are gonna be about $4,000. Materials will be pretty negligible per unit, but figure $600 to get going. Handwork, crafting, molding and finishing will be about another $2,500 for let's say, twenty units. So, I'd say you're looking at somewhere between $8,000 and $10,000.

Brando

That's a lot of money. That's like $500 per unit or something like that.

Anthony

Right, but once you get past the initial cost, you're looking at probably just a couple of bucks per unit without the microphone of course. How much are the mikes going for?

Brando

If I buy fifty or more per order, they'll be $65 each. Not cheap, but then they are very fine instruments. German-made. I heard the Russians order them for surveillance devices.

Anthony

Wow!

Brando

Is there any way to shave 25% off the top?

Anthony

Not with this design. You see, this is an acoustic study of the materials. The exact weight and composition of the materials are analyzed. I have to stick to these specs or they'll blame it on me if it doesn't sound right. Then you'll have real problems. I can't deviate from these plans. But I'll cut where I can. Don't worry, I'll be fair. I'd like to do this job. And we could mass produce them too.

Brando

Yeah, there is nothing like it. What about terms?

Anthony

This is all custom work. So we'll need half on signing, a quarter on plan approval, and the last quarter on delivery.

Brando

What about a time frame?

Anthony

Six weeks, eight at the most. I'll cost it out and send it to you or Hoffman, whatever you prefer. I can get right on this. You can have a quote in a week.

Brando

Good. Send it to me. Here's my card. Better send Hoffman a copy, because he'll need to document the disbursement for it.

Anthony

Fine. No problem. So tell me…how did you get this idea in the first place?

Brando

I always liked to invent things. My father was a tinkerer too. I take after him in this regard. We went to the same military academy and they have a trade school program so I think I caught the bug in that program. It's not rocket science. It's just something functional and there is a niche market for it. If it pays for itself, I'll be happy.

Anthony

Okay.

Brando

Do you remember Hedy Lamarr, the actress?

Anthony

Sure. She was a real beauty.

Brando

She had brains too. I got inspired by her. Did you know that she invented the machine that causes tissue paper to pop up out of the box after you pull the first one out? You know what I mean?

Anthony

Of course I do. Wow! That's amazing!

Brando

And she invented a design for the shape and position of high heel shoes to prevent ankle injuries.

Anthony

Wow! No kidding.

Brando

And even more amazing. She invented some kind of marine sonar for ships or subs for the Navy. It's very technical and I don't understand it, but she donated the entire project to the war effort and received a medal from the Secretary of the Navy.

Anthony

I had no idea. Wow!

Brando

And all the time we were looking at her tits.

Anthony

Great tits! Did you make a movie with her?

Brando

No, but I wish I had. She's still around somewhere. I heard she's not well but spends her time tinkering still.

Anthony

Wow, can you imagine the things she's come up with?

Brando

With a mind like that, who can. So in a way, Hedy was my inspiration.

Anthony

I can see why. Very impressive.

Tammy enters carrying the B volume of World Book Encyclopedia.

Tammy

Daddy, what is this word? Or-gee. She ignores Brando completely.

Anthony

Let's see it sweetie. *He has her point to the word as he takes the book in his hands.* What word? Oh, orgy. Ah, let's see, ah, I think it means something like a…a party. Yeah, a party between three or more consenting adults.

Tammy

Like a birthday party?

Anthony

Yeah, just like a birthday party.

Tammy

So, I'm going over to Brittany's for an orgy?

Anthony

No, no. You are not consenting adults. You're kids, so it's a birthday party only, okay?

Tammy

Okay

Anthony

Tammy, will you say hello to Mr. Brando?

Tammy

Okay

Brando

Hello Tammy. You can call me Bud. All my friends call me Bud and now we're friends too.

Tammy

Okay, Bud.

Brando

May I see your book? What subject were you reading about?

Tammy

Here, I was reading here, right here. Bacchus or something like that.

Brando

Let's see. Oh, the feast of Bacchus; bacchanalia, a Roman festival celebrating the Goddess Dionysus. Very interesting. Do you enjoy reading the encyclopedia?

Tammy

Yes.

Brando

You started with the A volume?

Tammy

Of course; it's the first one.

Brando

Yes, it is. Tell me. Can you look me up to see if I'm in there too?

Tammy

You're in here?

Brando

Yes, I'm just curious to know if they have me in there. Here, let's sit down together and do it together. *They sit on the sofa and she opens the book.* B-R-A-N-D-O. Got it?

Tammy

Not so fast!

Brando

I'm sorry. Again. B-R-A-N-D-O.

Tammy

Fumbling with the pages. Here it is. Hey, that's not you!

Brando

Let me see. *He takes the book and looks closely at it.* That's me alright. That's a picture from the movie, *The Wild One.* The sunglasses make it hard to tell and I was a lot younger then. But that's me.

Tammy

She begins to read the entry. "Marlon Brando, Jr., American stage and film actor, born in Omaha, Nebraska April 3, 1924; son of Marlon and Dorothy Brando."

Brando

You're a good reader Tammy. Better than me when I was 12. Congratulations.

Tammy

Thanks, Bud.

Anthony

That's the first time we met anybody in the encyclopedia, huh Tammy?

Tammy

Yeah daddy. Wait until I tell Brittany.

Anthony

Brittany is Tammy's best friend. She's gonna be 7 on Saturday.

Tammy

Her birthday is Sunday, but her birthday party is on Saturday.

Brando

That's nice. Wish her a happy birthday for me too, will ya?

Tammy

Okay Bud. Daddy's taking me shopping for a birthday present after you leave.

Brando

He is? Well then, I don't want to stay for too long do I?

Tammy

No.

Brando

Okay, but before I go, Tammy, can I ask you for a little favor?

Tammy

What?

Brando

I'm kind of hungry because I skipped breakfast like a bad boy.

Tammy

Yeah, you're bad Bud.

Brando

So, I was thinking…hoping…that I could eat a bowl of Cheerios with you before I go. Can we do that?

Tammy

Okay.

Anthony

I'm not sure we have any Cheerios left. Do we honey?

Tammy

Yeah, we got lots of them. Mom keeps extra boxes up there.

She points to a raised cabinet.

Up there, daddy.

Anthony

Let's take a look. Hey, we're in business. Two boxes. *He brings one down.* My wife's emergency stash I see.

Brando

What do you expect from an emergency nurse?

Anthony

Yeah, you're right. *The phone rings.* I'll get it. Hello? Hi honey, your ears must have been ringing. We were just talking about you. Tammy showed me your secret Cheerios stash. We're gonna sit down and enjoy a bowl together. *He listens.* Yes, Mr. Brando too. And Tammy, yes, of course. *He listens.* Really, you're all done already? That was fast. Oh, they're rescheduling it for another day. That's good. Come home quickly and you can meet our guest. But stop at the market first and get a gallon of milk. We need it. Oh, and a couple of bottles of pineapple juice too. Okay? See you soon. Bye. See Tammy, mom will be home soon. Please Bud, let's take a seat at the table. *They sit at the table while Anthony sets out bowls and cups, pours the Cheerios and milk, etc.*

Brando

I'm looking forward to this.

Tammy

Me too.

Anthony

Me three. *He sits at the table and they begin eating.*

Brando

Tammy, did you know that when I was a kid, Cheerios were called Cheerioats?

Tammy

Really?

Brando

Yeah, they got sued or something and had to change the name.

Anthony

Wow. That's interesting!

Tammy

It's my favorite cereal in the whole world!

Brando

He downs a spoonful. Mine too!

They all laugh and feast on their bowls of Cheerios.

THE END

List of Words Starting with the Letter B:

Babar, Babbitt, Babbler, Babel, Babi Yar, Baboon, Baby, Babylon, Babylonia, Baer, Bacchus, Bach, Back, Backgammon, Bacon, Bacteria, Bacteriology, Baden-Baden, Badger, Badlands, Badminton, Joan Baez, Baffin, Ireland, Baghdad, Bagpipe, Bahamas, Bahrain, Bait, Bailey, John Logia Board, Baja, California, Howard Baker, Jonnie Baker, Josephine Baker, Baking, Baking Powder, Baku, Battle of Balaklava, Balance, George Balanchine, Balboa, Bald Eagle, Baldness, Ball, Ball Bearing, Ballad, Balart, Ballet, Ballistics, Balloon, Ballot, Ball point pen, Balm, Balsa, Balsam, Baltic Sea, Baltimore, Balzac, Bamboo, Banana, George Bancroft, Band, Bandage, Bandicoot, Bandit, Banding, Banff, Bangalore, Bangkok, Bangladesh, Bangor, Bangui, Banjo, Bank, Bankruptcy, Bannister, Backburner, Banshee, Bantu, Banyan tree, Baobab, Baptism, Baptist, Bar, Barcode, Bar mitzvah, Barber, Barbados, Barbarian, Barbosa, Barbecue, Barbed wire, Bar bell, Barker, Barberry, Barbershop, Barbiturate, Barcelona, Barents Sea, Barge, Bari, Barium, Baroque, Barracuda, Barrel, Janis Barrie, Ethel Barrymore, John Barrymore, Lionel Barrymore, John Bartlett, Base, Basket, Bass, Bassoon, Bastille, Bat, Bat mitzvah, Bath, Bathsheba, Baton, Baton Rouge, Battalion, Battenberg, Battering ram, Battery, Battle Creek, Battle Hymn of the Republic, Battleship, Bauhaus, L. Frank La Baum, Bauxite, Bavaria, Bay, Bay of Bengal, Bay of Fundy, Bay of Pigs, Bay Rum, Bayberry, Bayonet, Bayou, Bazaar, Bazooka...

Up From the Ashes

Up from the Ashes

A local historical society meets for the purpose of re-invigorating its membership

TIME: The recent past

PLACE: The Players Playhouse, Detroit

SETTING: The playhouse stage is arranged with a head table and podium in the same manner as it is when Players meetings are conducted. The audience thus becomes the attendees of the meeting that makes up the action of the entire play.

CHARACTERS:

The Chairman: A distinguished elderly gentleman.

A Voice: Various members of the audience who respond verbally to remarks of the speakers.

Vernon Fisher: Similar to the chairman.

Oscar Findley: Also similar to the chairman.

NOTE: *The title is derived from one of the two Latin mottoes on the Great Seal of the City of Detroit: "It shall rise from the ashes." The play is a loving if not slightly over the top portrayal of the first meeting of the re-organized and re-energized formerly defunct fraternal organization called the Society for the Recovery and Preservation of Detroit Myths & Legends. The purpose of the Society is to foster a "Keener sense of local patriotism" in the community at large.*

The very notion of such a mission may appear to some as absurd but to the members present, it is a noble undertaking. The playwright hopes the sentiments expressed herein will become more than just mildly amusing.

*   *   *

Chairman

Hammer gavels on the podium.

Gentlemen will you kindly take your seats. I am determined to chair punctual and efficient meetings so let's get started without delay. Please be seated so we may begin.

Attendees become seated.

That's right fill up the front rows first.

Pauses.

Good, very good. Will our speaker please join me at the head table? Good, very good. Now gentlemen, it is my distinct pleasure to convene this meeting of the Society for Recovery and Preservation of Detroit Myths & Legends, the first general meeting of this August body in thirty-eight years. As your chairman I offer my hearty welcome and heartfelt congratulations to each of you, especially those of you who have renewed your memberships after so long an interregnum. Let's raise a glass to our beloved society: "Cheers!"

Voice

Hear, hear!

Chairman

My sentiments exactly. And to those of you who are new recruits, I offer my sincere thanks for your vote of confidence in the vision of us elder recoverees and preservationists. We trust you will find here what we found here in simpler times, namely a keen sense of appreciation of our fair city's forgotten and neglected history and heritage. Lord knows it is a noble undertaking.

Voice

Hear, hear!

Chairman

...*continuing*...

Let me also express my gratitude that you have selected me to chair the Society's functions until, of course, we conduct elections to seat a new board of trustees to begin the New Year. I trust many of you will be eager to give of yourselves unselfishly. Remember we ask only your time and enthusiasm as a generous bequest from our dearly departed Herbert Sloan Kerchival has happily eliminated our need to seek donations of a monetary character. Over the ensuing years his donation has quietly grown into a considerable endowment and we are proud to be the custodians of so large a sum. Herbert may you long rest in peace.

Voice

Hear, hear!

Chairman

Now without further delay I am delighted to call upon one of our most distinguished members to introduce this evening's speaker. So please join me in welcoming Mr. Vernon Fisher to the podium, Vernon? If ever a fellow recoveree deserved applause, it is he.

Fisher

Thank you Wesley and thank you gentlemen for your votes of confidence in choosing to support our dear society. During our cocktail hour I was truly delighted to make the acquaintance of so many new and ardent followers of our important mission. And in this age of bustle and distraction, it is a noble devotion. If you'll permit me to offer a brief observation, I'll just say this to remind you why our dear society was founded. Beginning with the rise of the automobile industry in the first decade of the last century, a massive influx of new residents necessarily diluted the number of those of us who found pride in our city's storied heritage. The loss of pride Emerson wrote is as stinging as the loss of one's granny. I submit gentlemen that the diminutions of our numbers these past three and a half decades and the resultant malaise it fostered will never become an object of our nostalgic proclivities.

Voice

Hear, hear!

Fisher

Exactly! The myths and legends of our fair Detroit (*French pronunciation*) are sacrosanct. They were inspirational to our great-grandfathers and they remain equally inspirational to each of us no matter that we often fail to acknowledge it.

Voice

Hear, hear!

Fisher

I thank my learned fellow recoverer for his vocal enthusiasm. What better way to honor our ancestors than to preserve the stories of their exploits in founding and settling their, our, city on the straits. For many of us it is a deeply emotional undertaking.

Voice

My sentiments exactly!

Fisher

Our speaker this evening is of course well known to most of you, if not all. He is a distinguished historian, author, traveler, and keeper of all things local and vital. He holds the prestigious John Chatsworth professorship of Great Lakes History at the University of Michigan and is a senior fellow at the Great Lakes Studies Institute at St. Michael's College in Toronto, and a long time and distinguished adjunct professor at the University of Windsor, which is situated beneath the awesome girders of the Ambassador Bridge. Among his many books is "The Frontier Metropolis," "Great Sons and Daughters of the Great Lakes," "Company Towns of the Northern Ohio Valley, "and "Red Settlers: Socialist Mid-Western Communities of the Early 20th Century". He is also an active member of national, regional, and local historical associations, having served on numerous boards and in many elected and appointed offices, including nineteen terms as president of The Algonquin Club, an organization we know well indeed. Tonight he will regale us no doubt on the subject of places names in an address entitled "The pointes and the Isle are Anything but Grosse". Please join me in giving a jubilant welcome to our very own, professor Oscar Findley.

Applause greets Professor Findley's rise to the podium.

Findley

Thank you Mr. Fisher for your warm remarks. I can assure you that your friendship is an abiding treasure in my life. Mr. Chairman, friends, gentlemen, I congratulate you for your efforts in reconstituting this important society for the present and future generations of our community. It is a noble undertaking and one worthy of our whole hearted support. I am happy to count myself among your honored legions.

Voice

Hear, hear!

Findley

Yes, thank you brother, I'm sure. Now, as Mr. Fisher stated, my remarks this evening will focus on a few of the stories of the origins of our illustrious place names. But if you will indulge me for a moment I would like to preface this topic with a brief note about the importance of local patriotism or what I call the nationalism of the neighborhood. I think you will agree with me that such a noble tradition is sadly lacking in our daily lives. What vestiges remain has been rudely transferred to our local sports teams or beer brands and the like. Gone are the days when the fierce Lower East Side Peddlers would rally an enthusiastic scrum against the proud Bicyclers of Highland Park. Gone too are the proud flags of yellow and red that once fluttered from balustrades that ringed the environs of both halves of Grand Circus Park, so named not for its semi-circular design but in honor of the temporary stables that were erected there to accommodate the grand circus animals that paraded down Woodward Avenue long before the formation of the Shriners Circus, which may have taken inspiration from the same, when it was founded here in Detroit in the late 1870's as a means of entertaining children and raising funds to establish our city's first modern orphanage-which was named of course after the famous African elephant Miss Stella and not as is widely believed after Stella Romanelli, the wife of Detroit's police chief in the 1890's, who was a big, loud, and loving Italian-American mother of eight was presumed to have endowed the orphanage with profits from her share of her late father's bread baking factory which was eventually acquired by Wagner Baking Company, which in turn invented Wonder Bread and which today sits on the southwest corner of the John C. Lodge Freeway and Grand River

Avenue in the present form of the Motor City Casino. Yes, it is stories like, these, little known as they are, that contribute to our local patriotic fervor. It is the loss of the same that appears to be a common malady of our times.

Voice

Shame!

Findley

Shame indeed. As we know from the massive and tragic conflagrations of the last century, nationalism is a particularly virulent strain of human pathology. If we surveyed the conflicts and ills of our world we can almost always find its indelible stain on the blood and tears of young and old alike. Nationalism my friends, and its half-brother patriotism, is the scourge of mankind. History proves this unassailable truth.

Voice

Hear, hear!

Findley

Yet when extracted to the lowest level of our civil hierarchy, nationalism has nothing but a positive impact. I speak of course of our cities and more precisely, of the subdivisions there of: our neighborhoods. By instilling a keener sense of local patriotism, not only is our collective pride elevated, but our streets are rendered safer, our local governments are more productive, our schools more effective, our neighbors more friendly, and our children, most important of all, our children, become more respectful of their communities and their elders. Lord knows anything that can take them away from their technological toys and put them in touch with the streets upon which their grandparents trod, the churches in which they were married, the institutions they founded and sustained and the cemeteries in which they are buried.

Voice

My sentiments exactly!

Findley

Clearly you are not alone my friend. So with that sentiment in mind I will devote the balance of my remarks to the precise topic of my address, namely the little known stories behind the names of places and routes of Detroit and its environs. Shall we start where X marks the spot, on this land beneath our feet? As many of you know, the historic and storied Players Playhouse sits on what was once a narrow depression that swelled with water in the spring and was known as Parents Creek. As you no doubt know from the state historic marker affixed upon the façade, Parents Creek was the reputed site of a massacre of newly arrived British soldiers by Ottawa Warriors engaged in Chief Pontiac's heroic but ultimately unsuccessful uprising following the withdrawal of French troops at the conclusion of the French and Indian War. But how, you might ask, did a seasonal creek under Indian and then French territorial jurisdiction become known as Parents Creek, "Parent" being a relatively common Anglophiliac surname? The answer to this riddle is deceptively simple. The French word for ditch is "per' an". To the average uneducated British draftee, it sounds a lot like "Parent" so Parents Creek" it became. Stories like this are rampant in our history due largely to the sudden changes brought about by the supplanting of the French by the British, and then of course by the evacuation of the British in 1796 upon the arrival of Col. John Francis Hamtramck. Indeed, the very name of this location on the river is evidence of this phenomenon. The Indians called it by various names including Negaunee, to the first French settlers it was "Detroit" meaning "upon the straits", then once settled it became Fort du Pontchartrain in the honor of the French Treasury Minister. Once the British took control of the fort in 1764 it was re-dubbed Fort Lernoult. And after General Anthony Wayne's arrival it became Fort Detroit, due to it being so dubbed on the out dated French maps he possessed.

Over a period of the next two decades, including the catastrophic conflagration of 1805, Messrs. Augustus Woodward, William Hull and Reverend Gabriel Richard collectively planned out a baroque styled radial diagram of the city environs beyond the fort stockades and the names they gave the streets and squares has largely remained until today. Note the generous use of French names like St. Claire, Gratiot, Lafayette, Campus Martius, St. Antoine, Beaubien, Charlevoix, and many others were preserved in order to placate the resident farmers of French extraction. Had they been made to feel unwelcome and left, no doubt the fort would have been abandoned due to lack of provisions.

Of course Mr. Woodward generously lent his name for our central zero-line thoroughfare and Father Richard was honored years later with the great park and a magnificent statue just east of our present location and across the street. And speaking of the park, those of you who have visited the Father Richard Park are no doubt aware that its eastern flank was utilized to base the northern end of the Belle Isle Bridge which was christened in 1927 but re-dedicated in honor of General Douglas MacArthur upon his visit to our city in 1952 following his infamous dismissal by President Truman as Commander in Chief of United Nations forces in Korea. Several of us present this evening attended the ceremony and remember well the general's gracious acceptance of the honor. A bronze plaque on the granite abutment memorializes that historic event.

And speaking of Belle Isle, how many of us know its original French name was Hog Island - yes, the French used that word because back in France pork was considered suitable food only for the impoverished masses. It was so named because the island was devoted to hog farming in order to segregate those noxious creatures from getting loose and devouring precious crops. It was renamed in 1840 in honor of Isabella Cass, eldest daughter of former governor Lewis Cass. Isabelle was a beauty, so she was called Belle for short, which of course is French for beautiful.

I could spend an hour on Belle Island alone but I'll mention only briefly a few of the monuments erected there to persons we once honored but have since totally forgotten, most notably Civil War Brigadier General Adolphus Williams, a loved hero if there was ever one. Williams Lake in Waterford is named in his honor but not a single boater or fisher would know it. Or what about the granite monument created to honor Robert Murphy, for his role in founding the Old Newsboys Fund. Or the white marble Nancy Brown Peace Carillon - recently restored - that celebrates the famed Detroit News advice columnist of the 20's and 30's and was paid for by her legions of loyal readers to commemorate 150 years of peace between the U.S. and Canada. Need I mention the Ann Scripps Whitcomb Conservatory, the Charles Flynn Skating Park, the Berry Gordy Amphitheatre and of course the infamous but eminently beautiful James Scott Memorial Fountain. I trust all of us hold a special place in our hearts for these prominent former patrons of our beloved city.

Voice

Yes, indeed we do!

Findley

And dare I count the buildings and institutions named after our fellow recoverer, the excellent Detroiter Henry Ford? No, I need not, I'm sure. Yet it was Mr. Ford who single-handedly created the city of Dearborn named after the famous fort that is now known as Chicago and carved out of Detroit the town of Highland Park, so called because at that time it was said one could see the river from the highest hill there. And did you know that the streets of Highland Park were named by suggestions of Ford factory workers? That's why so many are named after matronly women's names like Florence, Myrna, Agnes, Gertrude, Ethel, and Hilda. No doubt these were the names of mothers and grandmothers of the lucky workers whose suggestions were selected.The Grosse Pointes, of course, were named to signify the size of the riverfront they abutted. The Park, the Farms, the Woods, the Shores were named to both lay claim to but at the same time distinguish themselves from the city of Grosse Pointes' allure to upwardly mobile Detroiters who preferred to locate east along the shoreline instead of north along the Woodward corridor. Grosse of course is French for big or thick, especially when referring to land. Thus Grosse Ile is a big island and Grosse Dame a big shapely forest.

And though our public parks are in a shameful state of neglect, we must never neglect the fact that Palmer Park, Chandler Park, Vandenburg Park, and Hart Plaza are each named after our former distinguished U.S. Senators. Or that the John C. Lodge Freeway, James Couzens Drive, and John R. Rd. (the R being short for Reynolds) are named in honor of former distinguished mayors. And of course, how can one forget to mention in the same breath that our Cobo Hall and Exposition Center is in reality a memorial to Mayor Albert Cobo who suddenly died during his seventh year in office in 1957 as the foundations of the structure were being excavated.

I could go on and on my dear friends but I presume I've made my point abundantly clear. A people who have forgotten to honor their forbearers will almost certainly forget to honor its heritage and history, much to its everlasting loss. The recent celebration of our Tricentennial in 2001 was particularly instructive. While I commend the spirit of the commission for rallying the masses of the metropolis, and for spearheading the establishment of the new Riverfront River Walkway, those of us who recall our 250th anniversary in 1951 know that Detroit's population in 1951 was 1.9 million. Please don't consider this as a complaint. Quite the opposite, I like many of you were delighted by the festivities of the occasion, and my personal congratulations to the Detroit Historical Society and the museum for their substantial efforts in spearheading the anniversary celebrations. The new Woodward Avenue Plaza it unveiled to commemorate the event is wonderful indeed and a nice addition to the University-Cultural Center Community.

So, I will end on a hopeful note. Our city seal contains not one but two Latin Mottoes: *Speramus Meliura* means "We hope for better things." *Resurget Cinerbus* means "It shall rise from the ashes." Let both of these mottoes be instructive to us: Better things await us; up from the ashes we shall rise. It's true Detroiters no longer practice the Chalmers Cheer; Birmingham has forgotten the name of Blick; Plymouth no longer pumps the Pilsner, and Wyandotte has abandoned its observance of the Winter Wampum Wonder Day…

Voice

Shame!

Findley

A shame indeed. So let us resolve my fellow recoverers and preservationists to do everything in our power to inspire our fellow citizens to take pride in their cities and their neighborhoods. Remember, every city street is a universe in itself. After all what is the purpose of pride but to be proud? I for one am proud to be proud! Thank you gentlemen. I raise a glass to our noble cause Cheers!

Chairman

Our thanks Professor Findley for that rousing address. I for one am doubly inspired and daresay I am not alone.

Voice

Hear, hear.

Chairman

Let me close in reminding our members that we will meet again next month to formalize our committee structure. So please come prepared to volunteer your time. Now may I entertain a motion to adjourn?

Voice

Move to adjourn.

Another Voice

Move to adjourn.

Chairman

All those in favor of the motion to adjourn... Very well gentlemen, until next month, good night and God's speed with you all. Up from the ashes we shall rise! Repeat after me: Up from the ashes we shall rise!

All

Up from the ashes we all shall rise!

THE END

The Angry Ashtray

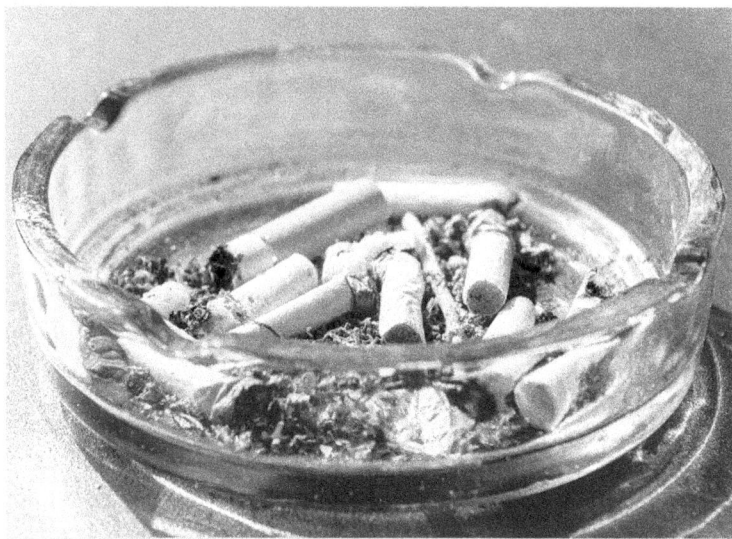

The Angry Ashtray

**An ordinary household object takes issue
with being taken for granted**

PLACE: Detroit

SETTING: A home's television den

TIME: The present (or somewhere near it)

CHARACTERS:

    Bob: Middle-aged male; portly and avid baseball fan

    Ashtray: (voice only)

AT OPENING: Bob enters the room with a bowl of popcorn
in one hand and a bottle of beer in the other. He is wearing shorts,
a sports-themed T shirt and he has his cap on backwards. He turns
on the television and makes himself comfortable in his easy chair.
An audio recording of a baseball game is playing on the TV in the
background.

*   *   *

Bob

*Reacting to the action in the game as he gets comfortable in a chair in front of
the TV.*

Yeah, throw them strikes!

Pause as he settles in to watch the game. Bob's cellphone rings and he answers it by saying...

"Okay, okay, okay, okay, okay."

He hangs up and returns his attention to the game on TV. He lights up a cigar and upon tapping his ashes into his chairside ashtray hears:

Ashtray

Your welcome.

He reacts to the voice, but ignores it. Again, he taps his ashes.

Your welcome again.

Bob

What? Who's there? Knock it off, Jim. Come on in and watch the game...if you promise to shut up!

Ashtray

It's not Jim. It's me.

Bob

Suspiciously...

Me who?

He grinds out his cigarette in the ashtray.

Ashtray

Ooooh, that feels good! Thank you.

Bob

What the hell is going on here? Who's playing a frickin' practical joke here? Jimmy, are you here?

Ashtray

No, it's not Jimmy old son. It's me, Mr. Ashtray.

Bob

Mr. Ashtray?

Ashtray

That's right. I say "Mr." because it seems to me you owe me a little respect.

Bob

I do? Respect?

Ashtray

Yes, respect. R.E.S.P.E.C.T. Ever heard that old son?

Bob

Of course I have. Aretha Franklin, The Queen of Soul; Atlantic Records, 1971.

Ashtray

Yeah, right. Whatever. Tell me, do you know Aretha Franklin?

Bob

Not personally, no.

Ashtray

Exactly. But you know me. Yet you pay her more respect than me. She's a stranger to you, yet you offer her her due because she's really good at what she does. Right?

Bob

I suppose that's a fair statement. All people are owed respect, if they earn it. Especially if they earn it.

Ashtray

Exactly. So don't I earn it? Day in and day out? Don't I earn your respect and admiration?

Bob

What?

Ashtray

Everyday you've used me for years. Did you ever think about me? Did you ever once think about the service I render you? A convenient place to accept your cigar ashes and your toenail clippings… and God knows what else you dump into me…without you ever giving it a second thought.

Bob

Well, I suppose that's true. I never really thought about it.

Ashtray

My point exactly. Consider it my duty to remind you that everything around you, the chair, the table, the television, popcorn bowl, everything…has a heart and a soul…and most importantly, we all have feelings.

Bob

Michelle!! I knew it was you. Alright, knock it off. Come out, come out wherever you are. What a joke. I gotta hand it to you, you had me going for a sec.

Ashtray

It's not Michelle, Bob. It's me, Mr. Ashtray…I thought we already settled that point. I thought we were making progress.

Bob

Making progress? What are you, a head-shrink? Feelings? Making progress? Oh, I see, it's Fair Play for Inanimate Objects Week. Isn't it? Great idea. Now, can I get back to my game?

Ashtray

Bob. Listen to me. I promise, it'll do you good.

Bob

I'm watching my game. Shut the hell up. Mr. Ashtray, right?

Ashtray

Okay. Fine. Ignore me. Watch your dumb game. See if I care.

Bob

Thank you. I'm certain we can talk about your feelings later.

Ashtray

Okay. Fine. I'll wait for a commercial.

Bob

Great. Thank you.

Ashtray

Starts to hum, like in meditation.

Hummmmm…

Bob

What? Why are you doing this?

Ashtray

I didn't say I'd wait in silence. I've been silent for far too long.

Bob

He raises the TV volume.

Ashtray

Aren't we mature.

It hums louder.

Hummmmmmmmm!!!

Bob

Okay, okay. What do you want me to say? Just tell me and I'll say the words.

Ashtray

It's not that easy, Bob. I'm not asking for contrition. What's past is past. Bob, I'm talking about understanding here, for the future. You get it? Understanding and respect. Put the remote control down Bob.

Bob

Okay, okay. I get it.

He slams the remote down on the table.

Yes, I get it. I take you for granted? I promise that in the future, I'll respect your feelings.

Ashtray

That's a start. Thank you Robert. I've been meaning to speak to you for a long, long time. Tonight seemed like the perfect time.

Bob

Why did you have to choose this particular game?

Ashtray

It's a long season Bob. May I have your attention?

Bob

My attention. What? Are you going to make a public service announcement?

Ashtray

You can think of it as you wish. This doesn't need to take long. So don't make it last long. May I proceed?

Bob

Yes, yes. PROCEED ALREADY!!

Ashtray

It doesn't need to be long and it certainly doesn't need to be difficult. So please grab hold of your emotions. This game of yours is totally irrelevant. In the scope of things, it means nothing. But your front door, your SUV, your bed and your toothbrush…now those things are important. Really important. Do you see why?

Bob

Well, I get your general drift. We do tend to presume the obvious. Like that the light switch will always turn on the lights. Things like that. It's true, now that you mention it. We take an awful lot for granted.

Ashtray

Exactly. I'm glad you're opening up. We're making progress!

Bob

Yeah, yeah. But these things you say I should be more respectful of are all objects that can be replaced. They're here for our convenience. Isn't that what a bed is? For our convenient sleep? Isn't my car for my convenient transportation? We pay for these things and we own them. So we really don't have to give them respect. Hell, they should be happy we bought them, instead of sitting on lonely shelves and dealership lots. How about respecting me? Huh? What about that Mr. Ashtray?

Ashtray

Bob, get off your high horse, will ya? I knew many fine slave-owners who used to speak like that. Then a little thing called The Civil War began and where are the slave-owners today? Huh, Bob? Where would you be without us? Without your cellphone, without your refrigerator, without your remote control?

Bob

Not my remote control.

Ashtray

Yes, Bob, even your remote control.

Bob

But I handle it with such care. It can never argue that I've been neglecting it, that's for sure.

Ashtray

Like my great-great-grandfather used to say Bob, "Touching doesn't mean feeling."

Bob

You had a great-great-grandpa?

Ashtray

Of course. He was a spittoon.

Bob

Now I've heard everything. Give me back my evening, you...you ashtray you. You dirty little ashtray!

Ashtray

Feel better now, Bob? Why don't you throw me across the room?

Bob

Don't give me any ideas.

Ashtray

Bob. Listen to me. The things around you are real. The street you live on, the office building where you work. The ice arena upon which you try to play hockey...they're all real and you should do your best to appreciate that fact. We're not the proverbial elephant in the living room, it's true, but we are here and there and everywhere. So don't fail to recognize us. You do so at your peril.

Bob

At my peril? What, are you threatening me?

Ashtray

No, Bob, no threats here. Just a friendly reminder. The next time you put on your shoes, the next time you drink from your coffee mug, the next time you open your laptop, just make sure you quietly give thanks every once in a while. Surely, a little gesture like this can't hurt you. Right, Bob?

Bob

Well, I don't see the harm in it. I suppose I can say thank you and please and all that stuff. What can it hurt?

Ashtray

Now you're talkin' Bob. Trust me, you'll feel a whole lot better knowing you're sensitive to the feelings of others.

Bob

Others?

Ashtray

Others, Bob!

Bob

Okay, others it is. Now, can I please get back to my game? We are having a hell of a season you know. I want to enjoy it while I have the chance.

Ashtray

Sure, Bob, I understand. In fact, we now understand each other perfectly well, don't we?

Bob

Yes, we do. Perfectly well. Later, Mr. Ashtray.

Ashtray

Later Bob. Just remember, inanimate objects have feelings too.

Bob

Got it. Bye!

Ashtray

Bye-bye Bob. I trust I can enjoy the rest of my evening too?

Bob

Yes, of course. In fact, I was thinking of quitting smoking anyway.

Ashtray

Just promise me you won't get rid of me in a garage sale, okay?

Bob

It's a deal. You got a home as long as I have one.

Ashtray

Thanks Bob. Good night.

Bob

You're welcome, Mr. Ashtray. Good. Night.

Bob turns the TV volume up. It's a commercial for Viagra.

Great!

Bob sips the last of his beer and looks at the bottle.

Okay Mr. Beer Bottle. Tell me, what is on your mind?

THE END

Bigger, Faster, Stronger

Bigger, Faster, Stronger

A glimpse into the hiring practices of a so-called "professional wrestling" organization

TIME: The Present

PLACE: Los Angeles

SETTING: An office suite

CHARACTERS:

> **John "Killer" Callaghan:** Wrestling Talent Recruiter
>
> **Harold Kowalski:** Referee Applicant
>
> **Frank Thorpe:** Wrestler Applicant
>
> **Murray Hunter:** Ringside Commentator Applicant

AT OPENING: The office of the Director of Super-Human Resources for The Big Time Wrestling Federation of America. A man is sitting at his desk behind a tall backed chair which is turned toward the audience so that he cannot be seen. He is John "Killer" Callaghan, director of the department that hires wrestling talent and other personnel for wrestling events such as referees, announcers, commentators and card girls.

*   *   *

Killer

Next!

A man enters carrying a folder. He is of ordinary stature, height and weight.

Have a seat please.

The man sits opposite of the desk. Killer remains hidden behind his chair.

Name?

Harold

Harold Kowalski, sir.

Callaghan spins around to reveal himself. He has an outrageous wig on, big dark glasses and a hideous suit of clothes on. In short, he is a spectacle.

Killer

Ah, there must be a mistake here. The employment office is down the hall to right. I don't hire the bookkeepers.

He points toward the door and motions his hand to signal that he depart. He then swings his chair back around to hide himself again.

Harold

Oh, I'm not a bookkeeper; I'm a referee. They sent me to you because they said inside-the-ring personnel was your responsibility.

Killer

Can you count to ten?

Harold

Of course.

Killer

Are you in reasonable good health and fitness?

Harold

I am, yes.

Killer

Can you feign anger, disgust and frustration?

Harold

I think so.

Killer

Can you travel up to three weeks per month of eight months per year?

Harold

Sure.

Killer

You don't have any problem with working afternoon and evenings even if they often last into the third shift?

Harold

It's fine with me as long as I'm being paid for the hours.

Killer

And you don't have a problem with being spat on, pushed around, punched and frequently knocked out?

Harold

Not generally. If it's mandatory that is.

Killer

Nor being ignored, disrespected, humiliated, booed at and otherwise made to feel like a fool?

Harold

I understand that it's part of the job description. I can take it.

Killer

Okay fine. What qualifies you for the position of referee?

Harold

I wrestled in high school; I've been a big fan of Big Time Wrestling Federation of America for over twenty years. Plus, my brother-in-law has been one of your referees for about twelve years and he has told me all about the job and has promised to train me.

Killer

Your brother-in-law? Who's that?

Harold

Pete Fontana.

Killer

Pete Fontana? Why didn't you say so? Pete is one of our best actors. That's what I call our referees, actors

Flipping through papers on his desk.

No disrespect meant of course. I call wrestlers "fakers." I wonder why Pete didn't provide you a letter of reference. That would help.

Harold

Because I want the job on my merit and not on my connections.

Killer

What are you crazy? Merit is dime-a-dozen today. Any idiot can be an actor, but not everyone has connections. You see we here at B.T.W.F.A. like to consider ours is one big happy dysfunctional family.

Harold

Sounds good to me. I came from such a family myself.

Killer

Will you be a team player Harold?

Harold

I promise. Yes sir.

Killer

Okay I'm going to give you an employment contract and non-disclosing covenant. Please read them carefully out in the hallway in the chair provided. When you're finished report to the office at the end of the hall with the big green dot on the door. Any questions?

Harold

What about pay and benefits?

Killer

They'll go over that with you and answer any other question. Okay?

Okay.

Now go outside and start reading.

He hands Harold a document.

Here.

Harold

Thank you.

He gets up and walks toward the door.

Killer

And Harold.

Harold

Yes Sir.

Killer

Always, always, always remember. All matters relating to B.T.W.F.A. are strictly confidential, do you understand?

Harold

Of course.

Killer

Where would we be if people think our matches are staged?

Harold

I understand.

Killer

Okay good luck. And give Pete my regards.

Harold

I will. Thank you.

He exits.

Killer

Bye.

He spins his chair around to hide himself once again.

Next!

Another man enters carrying a folder. He is big, tall and well built.

Have a seat please. Name?

Frank

Franklin Thorpe but everybody calls me Frankie T.

Callaghan spins around to reveal himself. He is now wearing a different wig and sunglasses.

Killer

Frankie T huh? Is that a broken or an inmate nickname?

Frank

Both.

Killer

I thought so. Can you fight?

Frank

Yes Sir.

Killer

Can you take a fall?

Frank

What's that?

Killer

Very simple, if you are requested to take a fall, will you do as ordered?

Frank

If it's part of the job, sure. As long as it's legit.

Killer

Are you crazy?

Frank

Ahh?

Killer

If you want legit Frank you are in the wrong place take your pick legit or paycheck.

Frank

Can I have both?

Killer

No.

Frank

I'm thinking.

Killer

Next!

Frank

Paycheck.

Killer

Smart choice. Do you have any experience?

Frank

Wrestling?

Killer

Of course.

Frank

Yeah. I wrestled in high school and I've been in about twenty Tough Men matches. I won most of them. That's why I'm here. I was referred by a guy who said he's one of your scouts. He told me to give you this card.

He hands Callaghan a business card.

Killer

Ah, Woody Lemon. Where did you run into him?

Frank

He tracked me down in Dallas.

Killer

Glad to hear it. That's his job. Do you have any injuries?

Frank

Not really.

Killer

Any health issues?

Frank

No.

Killer

Any problems with blood, spit, or puke?

Frank

Not unless it goes in my mouth or eyes.

Killer

I see you are the sensitive type.

Frank

I've never been called sensitive before.

Killer

This is the big leagues Frankie. A staged match can be more dangerous than a real one, apart from all the mental degradation.

Frank

It can?

Killer

Sure it can. If you go off you can wind up in the hospital faster than a gunshot victim.

Frank

How's that?

Killer

Because we have our own ambulance service of course.

Frank

Oh, that's good to know.

Killer

We take care of our crew because we invest a lot of money into them.

Frank

That's good to know too.

Killer

So the question becomes — are you worthy of our money investment in you too?

Frank

I think so. I have ambitions to become a world champion.

Killer

You do, do you?

Frank

Yeah I've always wanted to wear one of those fancy belts.

Killer

Uh huh. Would you have a problem getting bonked in the head by one of those belts?

Frank

Not if it means having a championship match.

Killer

Do you have a problem getting booed?

Frank

Do I have to?

Killer

Are you kidding?

Frank

Well if I have to.

Killer

You have to see everybody does. I actually like it. I like when the fans go crazy over a wrestler. In fact, that is the key to our success. in this business: you gotta find a way to connect with the fans. Hulk Hogan did it. The Rock did it, John Cena did it.

Frank

That's because they were always good guys.

Killer

Not always they weren't.

Frank

No?

Killer

Not at all. We need characters; that's what I am looking for. The bigger, faster, stronger guy is the one who will earn the most money. You get it?

Frank

I think so. I'm a character, I think.

Killer

Tell me about Frankie T. Where does he come from? What does he stand for?

Frank

Uh. —

Killer

When you figure that out, call me back. Here's my card with my private phone number on it. Think about yourself as a character. Pretend you are an actor playing a role. Here are a couple of scripts for you to practice on, (*hands some document*). Practice your most menacing tone. Act tough and fearless. Master that and you are in.

Frank

Okay, I will.

Killer

After you pass the characterization phase we'll send you to our gym to see what you made of see what you're made of. We'll sweat the truth out of you. If you look good in the ring, we'll schedule you for some matches of which you will lose everyone - gracefully I might add.

Frank

Okay when can I win?

Killer

When the big boss says so. Any other questions?

Frank

What about pay?

Killer

Compensation and benefits will be discussed after you pass phase one.

Frank

Okay. What about the time frame?

Killer

That's totally up to you. We always need good characters. Sometimes we need a bad guy with a big mouth. Other times we may need a tag team partner or an act for comedy effect. Perhaps a goon with an inferiority complex. It's not rocket science. It's entertainment.

Frank

I understand.

Killer

That's why we do villains, big-mouths, nut cases, hillbillies, Russians, A-rabs, you name it - and anybody else who can make a spectacle of him or herself. If you have a sense of shame, we're not interested.

Frank

So that's the formula.

Killer

You betcha. And it works; the proof is in the ratings.

Frank

I hope I can make you proud.

Killer

Just make me money and I'll be happy. Any more questions?

Frank

Um…no I don't think so.

Killer

Work on developing a strong unique character. Study the script and call me in two weeks.

Frank

Sounds good.

In character.

"Next time I see you Killer it'll be too soon. I've been thinking long and hard about the number of ways I'm gonna cause you pain. And you know what?

He holds up a piece of paper.

I've got a long list of 'em." How's that?

Killer

Fantastic, you get the idea. Now run along and practice practice, practice. Our best stars are those who can work a microphone from the center of the ring.

Frank

And can remember their lines.

Killer

You catch on quickly. Now exit quickly. I've got others waiting to see me, Hopefully one or two will be round girls. We're launching a line of bikinis so we'll be doing a runway fashion show kind of thing between matches to spice things up. We got the beef now we're gonna have the babes.

Frank

Wow. I can't wait!

He rises from his chair.

Killer

Call me in exactly two weeks. And always, always, always, remember that all matters related to B.T.W.F.A. are strictly confidential.

Frank

Okay Sir. I will (*In character*) "I'm gonna make you proud. I promise you real proud. "

He exits.

Killer

Fat chance.

He spins his chair around.

Next.

A tall slender man enters carrying a folder.

Take a seat please. Name?

Murray

Murray Hunter.

His voice is rich and deep, like a deejay.

Killer

Still hidden behind the back of his chair.

I'm not being rude Murray. I just went to take in the timbre of your voice without being prejudiced by your mug. Okay?

Murray

Okay.

Killer

Let me hear you recite the Pledge of Allegiance. Go ahead.

Murray

Clears his throat

"I pledge allegiance to the flag of the United States of America..."

Killer

He spins around to reveal himself. Once again he is wearing a different wig and sunglasses.

Pretty good Murray. You'd be surprised how many guys don't know it.

Murray

Thank you. I'm surprised I remember it myself.

Killer

You're a true patriot. Can you travel three out of four weeks seven months a year.

Murray

Yeah, no problem.

Killer

Can you do interviews?

Murray

Sure can. Plus, I do great phony outrage.

Killer

How about ringside commentary? I'm looking for color commentators with strong sycophantic tendencies. They need to be forceful and articulate on cue.

Murray

I'm certain I can handle it. I've been a fan of Big Time Wrestling since I was a kid. I feel as though I was born to join your ranks in some capacity or other. Not only do I possess a solid knowledge of your past glories and current success. I also pride myself on being able to help you develop strategies for future greatness.

Killer

Really? In what way?

Murray

The way I see it, Big Time Wrestling is equal parts sporting event, sit com and soap opera…and I mean that it is glowing positive way. It's that way inside and outside the ring. It's interactive theater and that is always fun exciting and full of audience participation. It's gotta be entertaining because that's what people want. That's what gets them to buy tickets and merchandise.

Killer

That's a good description go on.

Murray

All I'm saying is that I'd like to contribute to the theatrical narrative as well. I've always been imaginative. I have a penchant for the dramatic, the absurd. In short, I believe I can be a great addition to your team because I "get it".

Killer

Sounds like it. When can you start?

Murray

Any time.

Killer

Do you have experience being on camera?

Murray

I was a TV weatherman in Oklahoma City for six years and I used to do movie and restaurant reviews for the station too. Plus, I've done plenty of radio and a little sports.

Killer

Sports? Where?

Murray

At my son's little league games and my daughter soccer matches as a volunteer. Ya' know. Just cutting my teeth, so they say.

Killer

Uh huh. Well, you're no Mean Gene.

Murray

I know it's not much but it shows where my heart is. Howard Cosell was my boyhood idol.

Killer

I see. Do you own a tuxedo?

Murray

I use to but it was out style so I sold it to a friend who is a member at The Players.

Killer

I've met a few of those guys. It figures. If you have a hair for the dramatic, why didn't you join yourself?

Murray

High heels give me blisters.

Killer

Yeah, me too. Any other questions?

Murray

What's the pay and benefits?

Killer

They'll go over that with you down the hall. I mean questions about the job itself and what's required of you.

Murray

I think it is pretty much straight forward. I just want you to know I will be a great addition to your team.

Killer

Develop strategies for hype; work on your superlatives and you'll do fine.

Murray

Does this mean I've got the job?

Killer

Well you come well-recommended and I like what I hear and see. So yes, you do. Here's a copy of my employment contract and confidentiality agreement. (*He hands document to Hunter*). Read 'em on the chairs provided in the hallway and when you're finished go straight down the hall to the office with the big green dot on the door. Okay?

Murray

Okay, Great. Thanks for your time.

He rises from his chair and prepares to exit.

See you soon I hope.

Killer

Right. And Murray, always, always, always, remember that all matters relating to BTWFA are strictly confidential. Do you understand?

Murray

Absolutely.

Killer

Good, now run along and start reading.

Murray

Okay Thank you.

He exits.

Callaghan picks up the phone on his desk.

Killer

Delores? Who else is waiting to see me? Uh huh. And a manager. Any models from the swimsuit agency? No? All right then send the manager wannabe in. One minute Delores. Is he creepy looking? Uh huh. What about his manner, is he weird or strange in any way? He is? How about recommendations? Does he have any? From whom? Bobby Heenan? Bobby "The Brain" Heenan? Why didn't you say so?

He hangs up the phone and spins around again behind his chair.

Next!

THE END

A Hard Way's Night

A Hard Way's Night

A rock band's reunion dissolves into a swan song performance

TIME:	The Present
PLACE:	Buffalo, NY
SETTING:	An old rock n' roll concert venue.

CHARACTERS:

>**Brian "Shaggy" Swan:**   Lead singer and songwriter of the 1980's big hair rock band The Hard Way; anxious, hopeful, and energetic.

>**Derek "Spanky" Kopchec:**   Lead guitarist and songwriter; withdrawn, short-tempered, frustrated, and unemployed.

>**Steven "Say Hey" Hanson:**   Bass player and second vocalist; easy going, lethargic, laid-back, and suffering from arrested development.

>**Andrew "Doc" Barker:**   Drummer; balding, mature, mediator of disputes, and now a dentist.

AT OPENING: Backstage dressing room of a grand old Detroit-area rock'n roll venue facing demolition. It is strewn with clothes, carrying cases, beer bottles, guitar cases and the like. Posters of old rock concerts adorn the walls.

All four members of The Hard Way enter the dressing room exultant at having just performed their first concert in almost thirty years. Each have long hair and are dressed in some variety of 1980's rock attire. Each also is carrying a towel for sweat relief and a bottle of water. They hug each other, exchange high-fives and otherwise act a quarter of their ages. As the action proceeds, each of them slowly wash up and change into their street clothes and pack their belongings. The din of a microphone on stage can be faintly heard and audience cheering and clapping gradually dies out. Throughout the action cell phones occasionally ring but they are ignored by the band members' increasingly earnest and heated discussions. It gradually becomes clear why they broke up thirty years ago, and why getting back together is a pathetic pipe dream.

*   *   *

Shaggy

Was that fantastic or what? What did I tell you guys, they still love us. Cause we still got it!

Say Hey

Listen to them out there. We can do a third encore. C'mon, let's do it. They're beggin' for it. C'mon guys.

Spanky

No, no, I'm done. That's enough. No more from me. Besides I can't handle all that smoke and noise. I held up my part of the bargain. Now I'm done, thank you very much.

He bows half-heartedly and then removes his wig and throws it on the table.

Doc

I agree with Spank, fellas. I'm dead tired. I don't have anything left and I have to work tomorrow. Besides, you know what they say in showbiz, "always leave'em wanting more." By the sound of it, we've done just that. I'm calling it a night; a career in Rock n Roll.

He also bows and removes his wig and tosses it on top of the first.

Shaggy

No way, C'mon guys listen to 'em out there. We can't let these people down, they're our fans. They'll never forgive us. Please, guys. Think of what they're going to write on Facebook if we leave 'em hanging like this.

Say Hey

Yeah, they are probably tweeting already what a great show. I agree, we owe it to them. Hell, we owe it to ourselves. Besides, I've got two ex-wives out there. I want them to eat their hearts out because my babelicious new wife is sitting right between them.

Spanky

From the looks of both of them they've already eaten everything else.

He laughs.

Say Hey

Very funny asshole.

Spanky continues laughing.

At least they cared enough to show up and support a good cause. It's more than you-know-who did. Laugh about that!

Spanky

I'm glad she didn't come. She dumped me when I got laid off the first time. Screw her.

Doc

I thought you already did.

He and Shaggy laugh loudly.

Spanky

Very funny. You're a regular Don Rickles. Only he had more hair. Ha ha ha.

Shaggy

Guys, let's stop all of this nonsense. You're all acting like high schoolers. Can't we all just get along? This evening is supposed to be about saving this old dinosaur of a theatre for Christ's sake. Remember what brought us together tonight. We were invited to rock for a good cause.

Doc

He's right fellas. We ought to be proud of ourselves not knocking each other down. We raised a lot of money for a good cause tonight. They rallied to save this old place and we've helped them do it. Just think about the first time we played this place fellas.

Say Hey

The Pistons were still playing at Cobo Arena!

Spanky

I don't think this rat hole of a dressing room has been painted since. Look! Here, The Hard Way played here April 1st 1982.

Shaggy

I can still smell the Stroh's and baloney sandwiches they served us. Remember how we slopped the baloney with mustard and flung slices on the ceiling. Look I think I can still see dried mustard up there.

Doc

Gross!

They all laugh together.

Spanky

Did you ever notice how many gross things feel good? Like scratching your ass when it really itches.

Doc

Or flossing your teeth until they bleed.

Say Hey

Or picking off a scab.

Shaggy

Or picking your nose.

Spanky

Or coughing up a gob of phlegm.

Doc

Or releasing a big fart like…..

He farts loudly and they all laugh and say in unison "Gross"!

Say Hey

Some things never change!

Doc

You can't improve on perfection.

He farts again and they all laugh loudly.

Shaggy

Okay guys, C'mon. Are we going to go back out or not? Let's rock this joint one last time.

Spanky and Doc

No!

Shaggy

Hey that would make a great song lyric. (singing) "Let's rock this joint one last time, baby!" How can you two turn your back on the possibilities? It only requires a little vision, a little hope.

Doc

We're not 21 anymore Shaggy. There's no fooling these old bones.

Spanky

And there's no fooling me. This is one-off Shaggy. Sorry to disappoint.

Say Hey

Well if that's the way you feel.

He takes off his wig and tosses it on the table with the others.

Okay lets' call it a night. It seems a shame. It's not too late, you can hear them out there, and they're still calling out raffle ticket prizes. At least there's an after-party.

Shaggy

And a Meet n' Greet.

Say Hey

Let's par-tay. Let's bring on the booze and broads!

Doc

Sorry fellas, count me out. I told you, I have patients in the morning. Starting at 7:30am. I need my sleep and I want to take a long hot shower first. My arms are numb and my back and shoulders are aching like mad. I'm a little out of practice after all, like thirty years' worth of rust. I'm not going anywhere but home. Hell I'll be a grandpa in another month.

Shaggy

Ah Doc. You can't flake out on us now. Please.

Spanky

I'm with you Doc. No partying for me. Those days are over; long gone. If it's not an AA-sanctioned event I'm not going no matter what cause. I made a pledge seven years ago and I'm keeping it.

Say Hey

I'm sure there will be a punch bowl or something.

Spanky

Do you know what they put in punch bowls these days?

Say Hey

Or 7-up or O.J. Don't worry. I'll keep an eye on you. Trust yourself man. Cut yourself some slack.

Spanky

Are you kidding? Would you bring lightening to a thunderstorm? No way. I can resist everything, everything except temptation. I'm gonna do what I did in the old days, I'm going to have a Western omelet, sausages, and a short stack of Big Boy's.

Doc

Thank God some things remain the same!

Spanky

Like ugly waitresses and retarded bus boys.

Shaggy

I cannot believe you guys. This is our big night. Our once in a lifetime reunion show, and you guys want to flake out on everybody. That's a crime!

Spanky

No, the crime was thirty years ago when you sold our publishing rights for next to nothing.

Shaggy

Don't start that again mister. They were my publishing rights and how in the hell was I supposed to know those guys were crooks and would go bankrupt?

Spanky

You should have got a clue when the advance check bounced.

Say Hey

He's got you there Shag. We got screwed too.

Shaggy

It was your uncle, our so-called manager who negotiated the deal in the first place. He found those guys not me. He told me to sign here, and I did. If you two weren't so damn high all the time or chasing skirts, maybe you could have paid attention to what we were doing. I was doing everything back then damn it. This would not exist if not for me.

Doc

We know Shag. What's done is done. You are an artist not an attorney. We don't hold it against you. If it wasn't for you writing "Slow Ruin" we would have never hit the charts.

Spanky

What good was it when we hardly made a buck on it?

Say Hey

We were all to blame. We were young and dumb and full of cum. We jacked it off like every other band. Hell I don't even remember the 80's.

Spanky

That doesn't make it right. We got screwed by the record company too.

Doc

Knock it off Spanky. We're all over it. You should be too. It doesn't make a lot of sense to drag an anvil around, does it?

Spanky

It's easy for you to say, you've got money.

Shaggy

And he works hard for it too!

Spanky

And some of us don't have to because we married into money.

Say Hey

Come on Spank, lay off. This is supposed to be a happy time for us. We never see each other anymore. That's why they call it a reunion.

Shaggy

He never forgets anything no matter how long ago it happened, ever heard of "letting go" Spanky? They say it is good therapy. Or don't they teach that in AA?

Doc

That's enough Shag. You too Spank. You guys are taking up where we left off thirty years ago. The universe has changed since then. You should too.

Spanky

Oh, I've changed plenty. But it looks like some of us haven't at all. When's the last time you cut your hair Shaggy? I'll bet you saved every pair of bell bottoms you ever vomited on.

Shaggy

How poetic. Maybe you should write a song about 'em. Oh, wait Clapton beat you to it.

Spanky

Very funny. At least my future is not rooted in my past like some of us here.

Say Hey

Stop it Spanky. Do you need to remind us what an ass you can be?

Shaggy

How could we forget?

Doc

Yeah Spank, what purpose does it serve to dredge up the past? And you too Shag. Don't think about us getting back together again. We gave it a good run for a lot of years. We enjoyed more success than most bands. We should be grateful for that and call it a day. I mean call it a decade.

Shaggy

I was just thinking. I mean we really sounded tight tonight. And they ate it up. Hell, we were the first hair band of the 1980's.

Spanky

That's only because it was 1978 when we started playing together. Nostalgia is a disease guys. The Stones are a perfect example. Their appeal is strictly emotional; there is no logic in it.

Say Hey

Hey motions are real Spank. You know what they say, "attention must be paid."

Spanky

They also say it's no use to kick a dead horse.

Doc

Fellas, I hate to interrupt but it's been grand. I'm all packed and ready to go. God willing we'll do it again in another thirty years.

Steven, give me a hug. You too Spank. And you too Shag. It's been real. Give my regrets to Broadway. I don't imagine I'll be reading about it in the society pages. If they still have society pages that is. Take care of yourselves.

Spanky

Wait up I'm coming with you. I'm hungry and this old place is haunted with the ghosts of far too many over-the-hill rock bands, for my liking. They can knock it down for all I care, I'm not senti-mental. Demolition crews need work too.

Shaggy

Guys please. Forget about the future. Let's savor the moment. Lis-ten, the raffle is over. It's now or never. Don't let this moment pass without another encore. It'll be our swan song. Think of You Tube and all of the hits it'll get.

Doc

I'm no longer interested in hits. I'm only interested in sleep, good-night. C'mon Spank.

Spanky

Later dudes. It's been real.

He high-fives Say Hey but ignores Shaggy, who turns his back on him as the two exit.

Shaggy

Unbelievable.

Say Hey

Maybe they're right Shag. Maybe it's best to leave well enough alone. At least we can be proud we ended on a high note.

Shaggy

Yea I suppose.

Say Hey

Besides, if you want to carry on you know you can. You're the Mick Jagger of this band. You don't need us.

Shaggy

Thanks but it's not the same. Every solo album Jagger ever released has bombed. No, either we are in it all together or not at all.

Say Hey

Well that's noble of you. But when I think about all we've been through, I can't help but believe this band is cursed and always was. Calling ourselves The Hard Way now seems oddly prophetic.

Shaggy

You're just superstitious and always have been. We could have been huge.

Say Hey

We were huge......in July and August 1981. Remember one day we opened for The Romantics and the next day they opened for us. That's something to be proud of.

Shaggy

Yeah I suppose.

Say Hey

We may not make the Rock n Roll Hall of Fame but at least we have a gold record and our names are on the Billboard's all-time greatest on hit wonders list.

Shaggy

Yeah, that's true.

Say Hey

Every band has personality clashes, artistic differences, disagreements over direction, and all that. Hell Joe Perry left Aerosmith in 1980 because he couldn't stand Steven Tyler. He came back a few years later and they're still together today.

Shaggy

Yeah, they are, I know…. but….

Say Hey

But nothing. Where there's life, there's hope. Don't be discouraged. Shit when Spanky screwed Erica I got over it, didn't I?

Shaggy

Yeah you sure did, once you surrendered the handgun that was pointed at your temple.

Say Hey

Hey, I was on downers.

Shaggy

Yeah, it's true. We were all on something back then.

Say Hey

Sure, any band could have gotten tossed off the Tonight Show for smoking pot in the green room.

Shaggy

Yeah, you're right. Ozzy got thrown off for worse.

Say Hey

Reflecting

Yeah, those were the days.

Singing

"Those were the days my friend, we thought they'd never end, we'd sing and dance forever and a day…"

Shaggy

You've been a good friend Steve.

Singing

"Thanks for the memories, of days with a friend, of nights that never end. We breathed the air without a care, on you I could depend. Thank you friend."

Say Hey

Okay I gotta go. Shannon is waiting. Let's go and par-tay! C'mon everyone is waiting.

Shaggy

Go ahead, I'll be right out. I just want to wash up and brush my hair.

Say Hey

Don't dilly dally! Hey man, you were great tonight, in case I didn't say it. Fucking great! The years have been good to you.

Shaggy

Thanks man. It's not the Maui Wowie. It's the Maui air. Promise you and our family will come and visit us. Please. You'll never want to leave, I guarantee it.

Say Hey

Hey man, thanks! I always wanted to go to Hawaii. Okay, get the lead out.

He exits.

Shaggy

I'll be right there.

He starts singing to himself pretending his hair brush is a microphone.

"Come on baby, get the lead out."

He pauses and then changes to a higher vocal key.

"Come on baby, get the lead out."

He looks around furtively and removes his wig and tosses it on top of the others. He picks up his gear bag and exits singing, again in a higher key.

"Come on baby, get the lead out."

He exits singing.

THE END

About J. Ajlouny

J. Ajlouny is an author, journalist, editor, and playwright residing in Detroit. When he is not writing, he is reading or engaged in research on any number of topics that satisfy his need for stimulation or escape. When these all fail, he can be found at theaters, museums, and concert halls, soaking up the art that is too often under-appreciated. Hey, somebody has to do it!

Fresh Ink Group
Independent Multi-media Publisher
Fresh Ink Group / Voice of Indie / GeezWriter / Push Pull Press

❧

Hardcovers
Softcovers
All Ebook Platforms
Audiobooks
Worldwide Distribution

❧

Indie Author Services
Book Development, Editing, Proofing
Graphic/Cover Design
Video/Trailer Production
Website Creation
Social Media Marketing
Writing Contests
Writers' Blogs

❧

Authors
Editors
Artists
Experts
Professionals

❧

FreshInkGroup.com
info@FreshInkGroup.com
Twitter: @FreshInkGroup
Facebook.com/FreshInkGroup
LinkedIn: Fresh Ink Group

Fresh Ink Group
FreshInkGroup.com

In this boisterous but sensitive drama, playwright J. Ajlouny looks beyond public image to find the heart of this young woman thrust wildly into fame as a sex symbol. Presented as a play-in-the-making within a play, *Marilyn, Norma Jean and Me* weaves biography with humor to explore the movie star's widely speculated plan to leave Hollywood for Broadway. The author imagines her innocence and vulnerability, her friendliness and loyalty, even as the public image threatens to steal her humanity. This play is a must-see or -read for fans of film and stage, not just because it is so good, but for its powerful way of finding the real Norma Jean in the legend known as Marilyn Monroe.

PUSH PULL PRESS
Fresh Ink Group
FreshInkGroup.com

Marilyn, Norma Jean and Me

A dramatization of the movie star's secret plan to leave Hollywood for Broadway

J. Ajlouny

Adventures in Leninland

An Intrepid Journalist's Quest to Understand a Place Once Called "The Soviet Union"

J. Ajlouny

The Red Poppy
Josef Stalin at Home

A Dramatization of Yuri Krotkov's The Red Monarch

J. Ajlouny

True Russian Adventures

PUSH PULL PRESS
Fresh Ink Group
FreshInkGroup.com

Adapted Russian Play

Ajlouny's Bard Plays

The Trial of William Shakespeare

A dramatization of the authorship controversy in which the audience renders a verdict

J. Ajlouny

Meet William Shakespeare

A superbly entertaining one-person play starring The Bard himself

J. Ajlouny

PUSH PULL PRESS
Fresh Ink Group
FreshInkGroup.com

Ajlouny's Word Books

Who Said That?

The Stories Behind Familiar Expressions

For Readers, Writers, Word Lovers, and Trivia Buffs, Fresh Ink Group Explains Whence Come Those Phrases that Color Everyday Speech

J. Ajlouny
Author of Figuratively Speaking

Figuratively Speaking

Thesaurus of Expressions & Phrases

Fresh Ink Group's Collection of 7,500+ Figures of Speech, Catchphrases, Idioms, and Colloquialisms Sorted by Meaning & Context

J. Ajlouny
Author of Who Said That?

PUSH PULL PRESS
Fresh Ink Group
FreshInkGroup.com

Whoopi
Likes Her Bacon Crispy

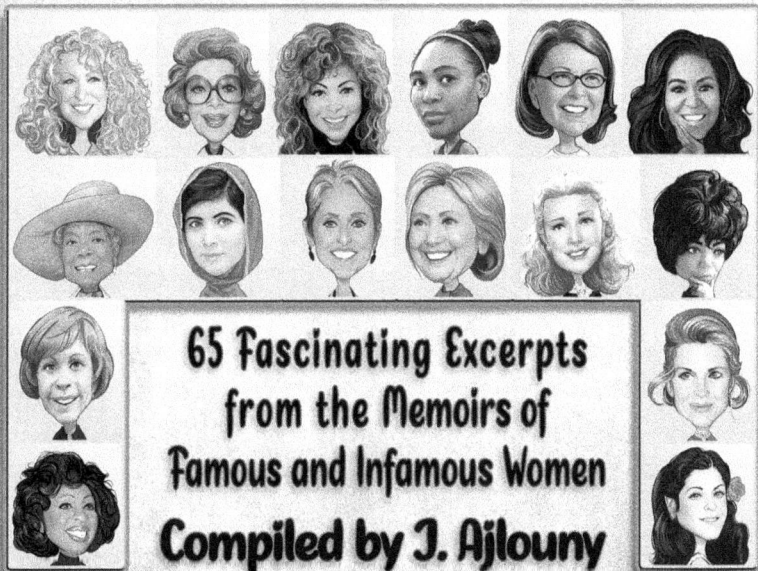

65 Fascinating Excerpts from the Memoirs of Famous and Infamous Women

Compiled by J. Ajlouny

Full-color Hardcover, Softcover, Ebooks

Fresh Ink Group

FreshInkGroup.com

If you ever find yourself on the Strange Hwy—don't turn around. Don't panic. Just. Keep. Going. You never know what you'll find.

You'll see magic at the fingertips of an autistic young man; a teen girl's afternoon, lifetime of loss; a winged man, an angel? Demon—? Mother's recognition, peace to daughter; Danny's death, stifled secrets; black man's music, guitar transforms boy; dead brother,   open confession; first love,
 supernatural?
—family be-
comes whole!

You can exit
the Strange
Hwy, and
come back
any time you
want.

See, now
you know
the way in,
don't be a
stranger.

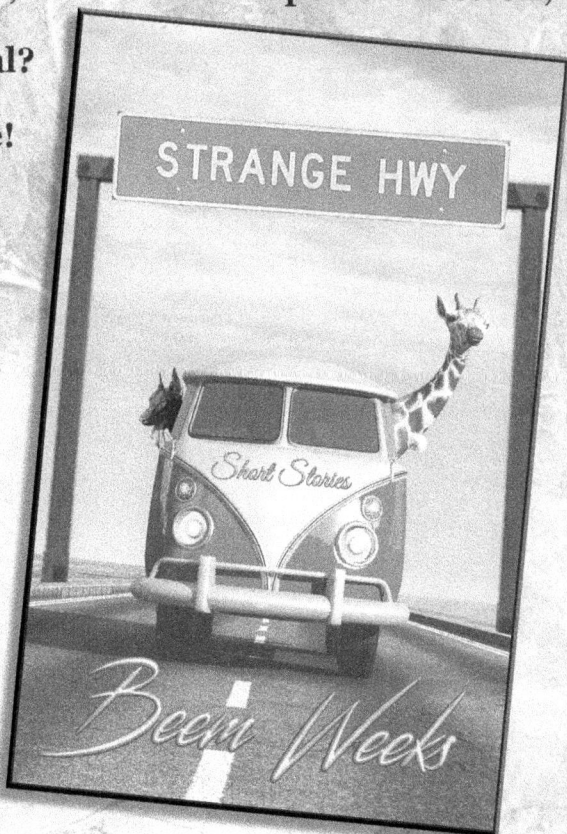

STRANGE HWY

Short Stories

Beem Weeks

Fresh Ink Group
FreshInkGroup.com

www.ingramcontent.com/pod-product-compliance
Lightning Source LLC
Chambersburg PA
CBHW051946090426
42741CB00008B/1290